Praise For This Book

"Really good book and one which I wish I had read years ago!"
– Garret Tynan, Infrastructure Banker, Ireland.

"This is a really useful book for any human who's not 100% happy with their relationship with money."
– David Stirling, Business Owner, Thailand

"I rarely bother with self-help books, but this one I will re-read, use and gift. The down to earth, honest and sometimes humorous approach to becoming more informed about your own financial situation is refreshing, and so important when dealing with the taboo topic of MONEY."
– Dr Donna Price, Teacher, New Zealand

"This book helped give me the clarity and confidence to own my financial situation. It guided me and made me feel empowered. I cannot recommend this book enough to anyone who may be struggling or even just considering a bit of financial guidance. If you spend your money on anything, buy this gold nugget of wisdom."
– Cam-Tu Tomkins, Educator, Canada.

"Fleur is a straight-talker and challenges the reader to be honest with themselves, with no judgement inferred. Because the book is private property, answering candidly allows reflection, insight and action planning. As a coach, Fleur understands that some of us prefer case-studies, others prefer exercises and others prefer to read and reflect. We are all catered for in this guide."
– Di Binley, Entrepreneur, United Kingdom.

THE MONEY PIZZA

THE SLICE-BY-SLICE
GUIDE TO BEING YOUR
OWN MONEY COACH

FLEUR IANNAZZO

**WTF!
MONEY?**

MAKING MONEY CONVERSATIONS EASIER

Author: Fleur Iannazzo; www.wtf-money.com
Editor: Wendy Yorke; www.wendyyorke.com
Publisher: Talking Frog Trading Limited
Cover Designer: David Ter-Avanesyan; ter33design.com

ISBN: 978-1-7385476-0-9 (paperback)
ISBN: 978-1-7385476-1-6 (ePub)

All names have been changed in this book for personal protection purposes.

Use this straightforward guide to change your money behaviour for good.

Contents

Language Warning

DID YOU TAKE YOUR grandma to see the film *Four Weddings and A Funeral*, thinking it was a lovely rom-com and were totally shocked by the first five minutes of swearing? Hmmm? Consider yourself warned.

Any uncited quotations in this book are the author's own.

Author's Note

THROUGHOUT THIS BOOK YOU will read many stories from friends and clients who have been generous enough to share them with me. All stories have been included with the kind permission of those involved. I have changed names and removed other identifying aspects to protect people's privacy.

It must be said that the information in this book is of a general nature only and does not take into account your financial situation, objectives or needs. Before acting on any of this information, you should consider its appropriateness to your own financial situation, objectives and needs.

But of course, you probably knew that already.

Vanessa, for turning my life upside down.

Jonathan, for helping me put it back together again.

May this book be the spark that lights the fire for you to have money conversations that serve you well.

How This Book Can Help You

Do you feel like you have been managing your money life pretty well so far, but something has happened to make you feel like it was all a fluke? Perhaps a child has blessed your life with endless love, body fluids and expense. Or, you have moved in with a partner and realise that you don't see eye-to-eye about money (and that's putting it lightly). You could be starting out on your own for the first time in your life, and want to understand what money actually means to you. Whatever it is, your old money habits aren't working for you any more – and you need to change.

Shifting your behaviour around money when your life is in chaos can be a particularly confusing and unspoken kind of pain. Everyone seems to think you're doing fine, but you are dying inside. It's hard to talk to someone who hasn't experienced it. I have.

With a solid banking career, I moved from low-tax Hong Kong to high-tax UK. I knew it would be a lifestyle step down, as a friend deftly put it. But I thought I was prepared for the income drop, believing it would lead to better career opportunities in the long run. Or so I thought. Within a month of arriving in London on my new career path, I was pregnant. A real SNAFU (situation normal, all fucked up). Every time I looked for support or advice, I received an answer on the theme of "It's never a good time to have a kid. You're earning plenty. Suck it up."

In the grand scheme of things, I had sort of planned for a child. Maybe. A bit. But deep down, buried under all the career success and lifestyle goals, I was not really ready for parenthood. In fact, I was so un-ready for it, that I had completely failed to plan, save up a Cash Buffer, or mentally adjust to the baby and parenting idea. I had always thought that people who had whoopsie-babies were irresponsible gits with no control of their lives. And yet, there I was - finances already stretched - and looking at one of the most expensive choices in my life, a child.

Cash crunched and bank balance racing to zero, I rushed back to work after a short maternity leave. On the first day back in the City, I trudged up the stairs to the office. The weight of responsibility to support my family and the chains of dependence on my banker's income grew heavier with each step. By the time I entered the office, I was gasping for air and terrified of losing my job. The pressure didn't ease. I couldn't admit that I was having problems with money because I had a job where I made recommendations about millions of pounds of investments! I indirectly managed other people's money. If I couldn't manage my own finances with this generous income, who was I to be in this job?

I knew our household was reasonably well off compared to the rest of the population, but we were still struggling. In fact, struggling seriously understates the effect our money worries had on me and my relationships. To cut a long story short, my anxiety about our finances and how I couldn't afford to lose my job threw me into a crater of depression. Just six months after returning to work, I had to take sick leave, and it took nearly a year to regain my mental health sufficiently to return to work.

So yeah, I know how money worries can hurt. I know that not being able to talk about money can make you feel isolated and alone. I know that people's expectations and image of you - because of who you are, your education level, or your income - can have a profound effect on whether you ask for help, receive it and ultimately recover. And I know it's not your fault if you are struggling to talk about money. Whoever you are and whatever you earn.

I also know that certain behaviours, which may have served you well in the past, are not helpful when your circumstances shift. These habits are tightly wrapped up in our values, identities, education and beliefs (along with a whole lot of other stuff).

And do you know what? I know how to crunch the numbers, and I can tell one end of a financial product from another. As a Chartered Financial Analyst, I am required to maintain an extremely high standard of financial knowledge. And I am dedicated to maintaining strict ethical standards when it comes to dealing with my clients, their money and the financial markets. In this book I share with you many practical methods - backed by extensive research - to help you change how you think about, and what you do with, your money.

If you are confused about money in any way - this book will help you understand it better. You will develop greater awareness about what money means to you and where you need to focus your efforts. It will also help you see clearly that money is not only about the numbers. It is about so much more.

I trust that reading this book will help you talk and know how you feel about money in a plain-speaking and uncensored way. No bullshit. This is the book that I wish I had, when I was struggling on my own.

How about we start by having some pizza?

Fleur xxx

CHAPTER ONE

What is the Money Pizza?

"Pizza makes me think that anything is possible."

Henry Rollins

LET'S THINK DIFFERENTLY ABOUT money. Leave aside all the usual stuff about spreadsheets and budgets. Instead, let's use a food analogy. And not just any food, but the best type of food. Easy, relatable and loved by almost all cultures. Pizza. Yes, pizzaaaaaaaah.

The Money Pizza is a discovery tool I use to start helpful, practical and positive money conversations. It helps people focus on what really matters to them. The great thing is, you can use this tool to coach yourself. It is easy to understand and will help you navigate different aspects of your money life more easily.

Using this tool can help uncover what is causing you anxiety around money and where to focus your efforts. It is also a great way to discover your blind spots; those financial aspects that you don't realise you need to think about. You will be able to see what needs your attention right now and what tasks you can park for later.

What's more, you will have a chance to reflect on your accomplishments. Believe me, if you have managed to reach the point where you are reading this book, you have already had a number of successes. They might have gone unnoticed or you may have downplayed your achievements. This book will help you appreciate how fabulous with your money you are already, as well as how much greater you can be.

There are pizza slices that deal with the practicalities of money and there are slices which look at how you think about money. There is no such thing as a perfect pizza (as I'll demonstrate below) and your rating of each section is likely to change depending on your current life situation.

Let's dive straight in. At the end of this book I will ask you to reassess yourself, but at the moment have a quick look at the Money Pizza.

Don't be too concerned about what each piece might mean exactly. What matters is what each piece means to you, today.

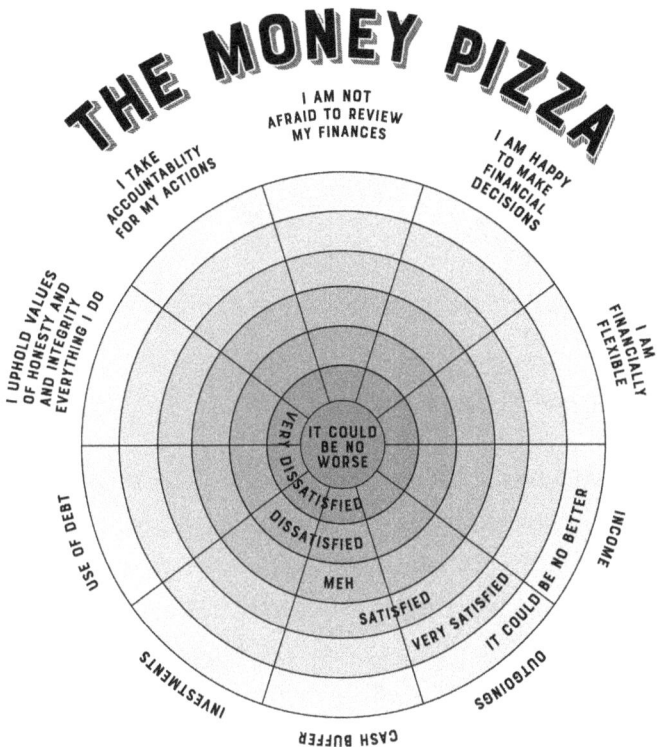

THE MONEY PIZZA

- I AM NOT AFRAID TO REVIEW MY FINANCES
- I AM HAPPY TO MAKE FINANCIAL DECISIONS
- I TAKE ACCOUNTABLITY FOR MY ACTIONS
- I UPHOLD VALUES OF HONESTY AND INTEGRITY AND EVERYTHING I DO
- I AM FINANCIALLY FLEXIBLE
- USE OF DEBT
- INCOME
- INVESTMENTS
- IT COULD BE NO BETTER
- CASH BUFFER
- OUTGOINGS

Rating scale (center to edge): IT COULD BE NO WORSE / VERY DISSATISFIED / DISSATISFIED / MEH / SATISFIED / VERY SATISFIED / IT COULD BE NO BETTER

Rate yourself on the following scale for each of the pieces.

1. **It could be no worse** - truly, it's completely shit and I don't know anything that could possibly make it worse.

2. **Very dissatisfied** - it's pretty f*@£$ing bad, but I do have days when I see how it could be worse.

3. **Dissatisfied** - I know it's bad, and while other people might think I'm doing okay, I feel unhappy.

4. **Meh** - honestly, dude, I don't know how I feel.

5. **Satisfied** - it's good-ish, but I want it to get better.

6. **Very satisfied** - I'm happy with how this is right now, but there are some things that could put the cherry on top.

7. **It could be no better** - everything is awesome.

The Money Pizza slice-by-slice

INCOME - this could be earnings, passive income or anything which brings in money that you can spend. If you have no income, you may still be happy with this slice. If you have a massive income but want more you could be very dissatisfied. It's up to you how you want to rate your feelings of satisfaction at the moment.

OUTGOINGS - this is more than budgeting. You could be very frugal and still feel out of control. Or vice versa. You could have one nasty habit that trips you up every time. Again, it's up to you how you rate it. Go with your gut.

CASH BUFFER - we will talk about what the 'right' Cash Buffer might be for you later. But now, you can gauge whether or not you are comfortable with what you have at the moment. Just one caveat - available credit on a credit card or overdraft does not count as a Cash Buffer. I'm talking about cash, cash, cash.

INVESTMENTS - I believe most people should have investments. But depending on your stage in life, you may not have had a chance to put aside much (or any) money in your investments. Rate yourself on where you feel you are right now.

USE OF DEBT - some well-meaning advisers will say that all debt is bad. I disagree. However,there are types of debt which are toxic and types which are much more useful. Also, it all depends on what you use the debt for (more about that later). If you feel anxious about debt, maybe rate yourself more on the dissatisfied end of the scale. Again, go with your own feelings of satisfaction.

I UPHOLD VALUES OF HONESTY AND INTEGRITY IN EVERYTHING I DO – I'm not gonna lie (see what I did there?) but I don't rate perfectly on this piece. For example: I fib to my child when things are difficult to explain. But what I really try to do is be very honest with myself about what I am doing with my money, how I earn it and where I try to use influence. Ask yourself: If you leave a restaurant and accidentally forget to settle the bill would you take steps to rectify the mistake? Or, would you consider it a lucky break, and you are entitled to a free lunch every once in a while? This is the only time that I will say there is a wrong answer in this self-assessment. If you rate yourself here as 'It could be no better,' you are lying to yourself and will enjoy a long and successful career in politics.

I TAKE ACCOUNTABILITY FOR MY ACTIONS - this is about how active or passive you feel about your life and your choices. Once again, it might be an uncomfortable answer to put down on paper but generally we all have room for improvement. Do you prefer to lay the blame on life, the universe and everything for when things go wrong (or right)? Or can you see where you have had an influence on the situation and how you might change?

I AM NOT AFRAID TO REVIEW MY FINANCES - this is pretty simple. Go now and look at your bank balance, your pension balance, your investment balance and your debt balance. Did you do it? If not, what is holding you back from looking? Now, rate yourself on this specific pizza slice.

I AM HAPPY TO MAKE FINANCIAL DECISIONS - would you prefer that an adviser/partner/manager in shining armour comes along and tells you what to do with your money and not have to think about it at all? We've all had that urge. But if this is your default reaction, you may want to rate yourself pretty low. Whereas, if you feel that making financial decisions is fun and gives you a sense of control you may want to rate yourself pretty highly here. On the other hand, if you feel burdened by your financial responsibilities, you may want to rate yourself a bit lower.

I AM FINANCIALLY FLEXIBLE - we all know people who feel trapped in their jobs because they feel like they can't survive otherwise. And it doesn't matter if you are a high earner or not - it happens. Financial flexibility is about having options - to pivot your life and leave an unhappy relationship; or start a family; or move to another country. It's worth having a look at this because inflexibility is often a source of much dissatisfaction with your money situation.

W ELL DONE! FOR MANY people, this is the first and deepest look into their financial lives that they have ever completed. It is a great warm up for the practical exercises later in this book. I hope you have a clearer view of your money situation right now and perhaps more of an idea about where you want to focus your efforts.

What money means to us

Before we jump to the rest of the book, it's worth busting a few financial myths.The first being that emotions have nothing to do with financial decisions. You probably suspect that money is more than a simple means of exchange. For many of us, money has symbolic meaning which often lies below our conscious awareness.

What's more, money is really emotional. Any decision we make about ourselves will be soaked in emotion, whether we acknowledge it or not. Money is often linked to how we see ourselves and our identities. The idea that you can

'take the emotion' out of money is bullshit. Be suspicious
of anyone who says they are completely unemotional
about money because it's impossible. Instead, you might
want to take some time to examine the awkward or
nonsensical emotions you might feel around money
issues. This is for one key reason: your emotions have a
direct link to your thoughts, and the way you think directly
effects your behaviour.

EMOTIONS ➤ THOUGHTS ➤ BEHAVIOURS

Making this equation more specific to money, you have
the following.

EMOTIONS AROUND MONEY ➤ THOUGHTS AROUND MONEY ➤ BEHAVIOURS AROUND MONEY

When it comes to money, it's not what you know, but how
you behave that matters. All the financial qualifications in
the world won't help you be better with money. (Ask me
how I know!)

To understand your behaviours, you need to look at
your emotions, and the behaviour patterns you build up
during your lifetime. Consider those emotional memories
– positive and negative – which seem to flash up at
inappropriate moments. The stronger the emotion, the
more likely it is to anchor a memory in your conscious
and subconscious. This has knock-on effects on your

behaviour, and you may find yourself in an unwanted habit loop.

To improve how you handle your money issues, you need to be willing to go deeper than the usual cognitive rational thought. You are invited to uncover what lies beneath. Sounds spooky right? But it isn't really. It's just a way to know yourself better. The Money Pizza helps you look at your behaviours, and your relationship with money so you can improve it.

Being a highly qualified financial expert doesn't actually save you from making lousy personal finance decisions, either. It's a bit like being a doctor and having unhealthy habits. It happens, right? We are all human. We are not aliens who can rationally parse all available information like a Vulcan in Star Trek. What sets us apart as human beings is our capacity for emotion, feeling and cognitive thought.

Traditional economics is wrong about humans

For decades, the dominant assumption in finance was that people can make rational economic decisions based on the information available to them. Any error in those decisions was put down to incomplete information. Somehow, economists dreamed up Mr Spock before Star Trek was invented. Spock's so called rational ability was probably influenced by the dominant economic theory in the 1960s, that the best financial decisions could only be made with data, and without emotion.

This view of economics was knocked off its perch when the Nobel Prize for Economics was awarded not once, but multiple times to behavioural economists. In 2002, Daniel Kahneman won the prize for Economics.But here's the twist – he is a psychologist who researched how people make decisions under uncertainty.

The first woman to win a Nobel Prize for Economics in 2009, Elinor Ostrom was a political scientist (again, not an economist) who researched how organisations govern themselves. Importantly, she investigated real-life case studies in several countries, rather than relying on pure economic theory.

Robert Schiller won in 2013, for his work on heuristics, which are the short cuts our brains take to make complex decisions. Heuristics[1] are often good enough in the short term, but perhaps not great for long-term decisions.

In 2017, Richard Thaler received a Nobel Prize for his research on decision making, self-control, and

---

1. 'Heuristic' (pronounced 'hee-yur-IST-ik') is a great word to whip out when someone is trying to impress you with their financial knowledge. Fire back a 'Yes, but what heuristic are you using to make that decision?' It'll shut most people up instantly. Alternatively, you might start a really interesting conversation with someone who knows their stuff.

how imperfect human thinking influences financial markets. He coined the term 'nudging', whereby certain environments can encourage people to make better decisions for their long-term self-interest. Thaler's ideas have been adopted in many areas of public policy.

This knowledge all came too late for me. I first studied economics in 2002 when the university I attended whole-heartedly embraced the traditional economic theories from the 1960s. Our frustrated left-leaning lecturer railed against the neo-liberalist pro-globalisation drive of business schools (including ours). His concerns were dismissed in favour of neat little graphs of supply versus demand, equilibrium prices and other dull concepts.

Needless to say, I almost failed economics. My saving grace was a guy called Richie who captained the local Aussie Rules football team. Built like a brick shit-house, he was good looking and had at least half a brain. The only reason I ever turned up to lectures was a chance to sit next to him. And he wrote great notes too, thank my lucky stars! Because I certainly was not paying attention to our cardigan-clad lecturer at the time ... but I digress.

The point of all of this is: if economic theories have never quite made sense to you, that is because they don't make sense to many other humans either. I could never answer an economics question well, because I just could not understand how 'rational' decisions were made.

I tried to understand economics again - almost a decade later when I studied for the Chartered Financial Analyst exams. Only then was I introduced to behavioural economics, as the banking industry tried to understand and grapple with the fallout from the catastrophic global financial crisis, which started in 2008.

However, decision makers have not yet caught up. As I write in 2024 we are now experiencing what happens when economists try to use rational tools like quantitative easing, to fix an crisis built on human error. Hello inflation, you old foe. Will we ever learn?

But enough about big picture economics. The rest of this book is focussed on real-life situations and real people, exactly like you, your brain and your wallet, as the following example demonstrates.

Fiona's Money Pizza Story

Fiona (37) a banker in the City of London came to me in a panic. She was in her late thirties, with a new baby and was struggling to adapt.

> "I'm completely stuck now. I can't help thinking that if only I didn't have a kid, everything would be fine. But now I feel like my husband and I are trapped in our jobs. The thought of unemployment terrifies me. I work in finance and have always had a good handle on money.

"We've saved a bit but it is not enough to be able to support a baby. I have no idea what to do! I can't go to work and demand to be paid more because I know that I'm at the upper end of the pay bracket. But I don't see how we are going to cope. How the hell did my parents manage to raise three kids on one income? I asked my mum, and she only said 'We had to pull our belts in'. I can't talk about it with my friends. Most of them have left their jobs to become stay-at-home mums. I don't feel like we have any options."

We sat down together to go through the Money Pizza slice-by-slice.

Fiona saw that her Cash Buffer (almost nil) and her Financial Flexibility (no options and terrified about unemployment) were her biggest worries. She recognised that whilst clear headed about decisions at work, she hated the burden of making decisions about money at home. And while previously, she had loved looking at her bank balance regularly, she now avoided it.

Fiona also recognised where her strengths were, including the facts that she was: in a good income bracket; financially literate; had a strong moral and ethical compass; and was determined to make steps to take control of her money situation again.

After an intense discussion, Fiona went from being overwhelmed and not knowing where to start – to knowing exactly where her money strengths and weaknesses were.

After her first session Fiona told me.

"I know in my heart that nothing has changed. But now I have spoken about my situation, and put it on paper, I feel much clearer about how and where I can start regaining control. I realise that I had a fixed view of what work would look like for me in my money life. Now I have a new life with a child, my patterns from my previous pre-child life need to change."

THE REST OF THIS book is going to help you understand your money story; to have more courageous conversations around money; and also, to make better decisions about how money can work for you.

The information in this book will give you the tools and the power to change your money behaviour when you want to. Equally, you may reach the end of this book and realise you are doing pretty well thank-you-very-much and it will validate your efforts.

Using the Money Pizza will shift the command and choice back into your hands when it comes to money.

By the end of this book, you will have strategically examined your money life and probably uncovered a few gems about yourself and perhaps change a few habits.

When you arrive at the last page you will have had important money conversations – with yourself or with a trusted friend. My goal is to guide you through these conversations with compassion and empathy and also a little bit of Mamma Iannazzo real talk. Think of me as that aunt who will always think the world of you, but occasionally tells you when you are acting like a pillock.

CHAPTER TWO

Your Money Story

"Until you make the unconscious conscious,
it will direct your life and you will call it fate."

Carl Jung

I F YOU ONLY READ one chapter in this book, read this one. This chapter will help you understand how your money story has formed, how it affects your life now and importantly, how you can change it. The information in this chapter can relate to your habits in every slice on the Money Pizza, so it's a great overview.

First, let me explain about stories. We use stories to shape our understanding about the world and about ourselves. They are a powerful tool to help us navigate our hugely complex environment – while at the same time maintaining our own sense of identity.

The stories we tell ourselves as we grow up form a large part of how we see ourselves – our strengths and weaknesses, our capabilities and potential. But here is the catch – stories are shortcuts and don't hold all the relevant information. We cannot possibly process all the data, facts and truth around us all the time. Instead we create stories around events which help us work out how to function in life.

Identifying your own money story is important because when you do so, you can choose to stop acting on autopilot. Just because you have always told yourself you will never be good with money because you failed Year 10 Maths, doesn't mean that it is true. It's a story. If you can identify some of your conditioned behaviour and then weaken the internal restrictions which are holding you back, your life will improve.

This chapter will help you understand that your behaviour today has been built up over many years. But even better, when you realise how your behaviour has been formed, you can change it. You will understand why this is, and it will prompt you to reflect on your own history to understand more of your behaviours today.

The most important message is this: no matter where you have come from there are changes you can make today to improve your money behaviours. That is not to say that everything is in your control – far from it. But there is far more within your control than you might realise. If there is one thing that you will be able to do, it is to work out where you have agency in your life. This means, where you can make a change and make improvements for the long term. You could even pass down these good behaviours to the next generation of your community.

Money habits form early

Our money habits are formed when we are young. How young? When we are striking out on our own? Teenagers? When we first receive pocket money? In 2013, the Money Advice Service of the UK Government commissioned University of Cambridge researchers to find out exactly how young we are when our money habits are formed. Their conclusion? Adult money habits are established by the age of seven.

When I read the research, it knocked my socks off. This doesn't only apply to money habits, but all our habits. Our parents and caregivers play an exceptionally important role in how we form behavioural patterns. We learn by mimicking them, and by unconsciously adapting our behaviours to please them. To an extent, we are also influenced by peers, teachers, media and advertising. But there is no doubt we depend on our caregivers for our survival and they are the single most important influence on our lives in the first crucial years.

If you are reading this with a sinking feeling in your stomach, thinking "Well that's me totally fucked for life", stop right there. Don't panic yet, there is hope.

While habits might be established by the time we are in Year 2, consider them to be set in jelly – not set in concrete. The shape is there, but it is wobbly and can be changed. Think of all the habits you have broken and made since then. Do you now brush your teeth without someone prompting you? Have you stopped picking your nose? Can you tie your shoelaces with reasonable ease? Right – there is proof you don't stop changing. You can learn new things and you can change your behaviours. But first, let's see why your care-givers are so important to how you act today.

You weren't born bad with money

Let me make one thing clear: there is no finance-and-money gene with which most bankers are blessed or cursed. Neither is there an identified gene for entrepreneurship, negotiation or numerical skills. In his outstanding book *Not In Your Genes: the real reason children are like their parents*, Oliver James explains that, due to our complete dependence as infants on our parents, humans have learned to unconsciously adopt behaviours which will ensure that our caregivers take care of us.

There is nothing inborn in any of us like talent, stupidity, humour, wittiness or a drive to succeed. There are no genes that explain differences in how we think. In 2014, Professor Robert Plomin who was the world's leading geneticist at that time said "I have been looking for these genes for fifteen years. I don't have any". Since he made that statement, research about the links between genes and our aspirations, thoughts, attitudes, relationships and personality has continued. A study of nearly 5,000 pairs of twins published in November 2021, concluded that genes form a 'nudge' for us to develop along certain lines. At the same time, the researchers acknowledged environmental factors (family environment, socioeconomic factors and personal health) explain many individual differences in these attitudes and personality. Genes are only a prod, and as with all behavioural nudges, we have the choice to follow that path, or to choose another one.

When we are babies, we learn to do everything in relation and reaction to the adults around us. We learn to wake, eat, relax, play and talk in response to the wishes of those big people towering over us. Caregivers encourage some activities and discourage others and children adjust accordingly – but not necessarily in predictable ways. There is nothing sinister about this, it is simply how we humans learn to live as social animals when we are so helpless for most of our young lives.

We naturally identify with our caregivers and tend to adopt their opinions and behaviours. In turn, they expressly teach and coach us in the 'right' ways of doing something – as well as modelling behaviour. Sometimes, they try to teach us by telling. But we must understand that as children, we learn by mimicking first. Only later do we learn by being told to do something. We develop our visual processing capabilities well before our verbal skills. Children are really good at ignoring the words, and copying the behaviour – as any parent can tell you.

Identify the unspoken

So much of what we learn from our parents, family and community is implicit. That is, the lessons are unspoken. We start learning those lessons far earlier than previously realised. (As an aside, parents; if you think you can put off the money lessons until your little ones are 'old enough to understand' think again. Their own understanding is forming as you read this.) The aim of this chapter is to take those lessons we learned early in our lives and make them explicit. Put them into words, speak them out loud, or write them down on paper.

It might help you to think about it this way: you can't shoot at something you cannot see. By bringing your money stories into focus, you can choose to dismantle or re-write them. It is also worth mentioning that as we grow and develop our own sense of identity, we may rebel and do exactly the opposite of what we see in older generations.

Recognising this rebellion in yourself is as important as recognising what passed down beliefs you have kept.

This is not an encouragement for you to tear apart your parents in an attempt to shift any blame onto them. Not at all. This is now and that was then, as they say. Nor should you pathologise any experience you have had during your childhood. This discussion is not here to stir up trauma or tell you that you had a shit childhood. It is not an exercise in blame or judgement. It is an exercise in observation. Try to remember what was actually there – not what you think was there.

You are encouraged to note what happened to you, without labelling it good or bad, right or wrong. Examining our past stories can be painful. Even when you remember a happy memory, you may also have a sense of loss. Instead, you are invited to look at your past stories with curiosity and interest – like you are watching a show on TV. Put things into context and treat your younger self and caregivers with as much empathy and compassion as you possibly can.

Jenny's money story

Jenny (34) is a senior executive in Bristol at a marketing agency. After moving in with her fiancé she realised that she and her partner did not see eye-to-eye in terms of how to manage their joint finances. Not to mention the wedding planning storm. It was causing so much tension in her relationship Jenny feared they might never actually make it to the wedding.

Jenny had an investment property of her own, and spent much of her disposable income on furnishings and clothing. She was clear sighted about what she liked to spend her money on, and she had no illusions about the amount of money that went into her shopping. Attempts to put more money aside to save or invest have always fizzled out.

During our money coaching conversation, I asked her to tell me how she learned about money when she was younger. Jenny explained that she had no formal financial education, and money was not spoken about in the household where she grew up. *"Except, of course, when my parents argued about it. It seemed like Dad earned the money, while Mum spent it"*. After gentle questioning, she recalled a couple of key moments around the time when her parents' marriage was under a lot of strain.

"Mum and Dad were in another part of the house, arguing about this beautiful sculpture mum had bought. She had gone back to university as a mature-aged student, and this was her reward for finishing. The only thing was, she'd spent so long coveting this sculpture that – by the time she graduated – dad had been made redundant and was unemployed at the time. I remember the crescendo of voices and dad yelling '... but I can barely pay the kids' school fees and you bought a bloody sculpture!? That's

worth a year of fees for the kids. What were you thinking?!'
Mum, of course, became defensive and there was no
option of returning the sculpture.

"I know I'm piecing this together with the benefit of
hindsight, but I realised that sometime after the sculpture
incident, they announced they were going through a
divorce. As these things go, there was a lot of emotion,
but Mum and Dad tried to resolve it as best they could.
Mum tended to demand everything and Dad tended to
acquiesce. They decided to sell the family home as soon
as possible. Doing so was a financial disaster – for both
of them. The market was terrible because there was a
recession on and they ended up making a small loss. Since
then, dad has always told me to 'Hold on to your property,
now is not a good time to sell'. I find myself wondering if
it's ever a good time to sell.

"Telling you this story, I've just had this realisation – I
spend money like my mum! That is, I'm very thoughtful
in what I buy, and I love what I have around me. But I
spend a lot of money – which is okay by me, because
I feel it's my money. I don't like getting rid of anything
either. On the other hand, I invest like my dad. I am too
scared to sell anything. And since my investment property
hasn't increased in value as much as I wanted, I don't want
to sell it right now – even if selling would mean that my
fiancé and I could put together a deposit for a new place
of our own. And, oh god! I've also realised that when I

think about discussing money, I have little flashes of the sculpture incident every time. I can already imagine my fiancé and I divorcing because of money arguments – and we're not even married yet! It seems so obvious now that I've said it out loud."

When you read Jenny's story, you might be struck by the power of her narrative. How much emotion, pain and suffering there is behind her words. The unconscious flashes of arguments that pop up when she and her fiancé talk about money might be causing her to automatically repeat the same actions and emotions her parents demonstrated. Not to mention, the parallels she recognised with both parents and their behaviours. Realising this link by telling her story, has helped Jenny identify when she might be falling into her own unconscious patterns and figure out strategies for what to do instead. Ultimately, Jenny decided to tell her fiancé her money story. She also asked him to talk about his own story, which she says has made it easier for them both to be frank about their financial concerns.

Looking at your money story can be really helpful, although also uncomfortable and sometimes painful. Give yourself a little time and space to do one or all of the following suggested exercises. You might want to complete them with a trusted friend or relative, or on your own. Whatever makes you feel more comfortable. Keep noise and distractions to a minimum, fetch yourself a drink of water, and settle into it. Write down (or say out loud) the words that come into your head as they do. Feel free to write down whatever appears for you. Nobody needs to read your notes and you don't have to re-read them either if you don't want to. Be honest and above all, be kind to yourself.

Exercise – Money Is...

Find a large sheet of paper (A4 or bigger) and pull out a pen. Write 'Money is ...' on the paper (wherever you like). Set a timer for five minutes. Fill as much of the page as you can with words which complete the sentence. Keep writing until the timer stops you.

- Have a look at what you have written. Do any words pop out at you as being odd?

- Are there any words which you didn't really think you should write, but you did anyway?

- Did you find yourself thinking about what might happen if someone saw your words?

- How did it make you feel?

What do you think this exercise has revealed about yourself?

Mine to claim

The answer + not the answers.

Options

Choice

Crass

Tic-Tac Time

Astable

Distracting

My daughter's future

Freedom

Not in myself

Difficult

Vulgar

Date

Savings + security

Eating nice things

Analysis Maths

Opportunity

Education

Sports freedom

English Fun

Skill + pain in the arse.

A bit risky. Exhausting

Within reach + just out of reach

What I want.

Taboo

Hours in the day

Embarrassing

Uncomfortable conversations

Never enough. Integrity

Like sand through my fingers (sometimes)

Other

Money is...

I complete this exercise all the time with my clients. Instead of asking them to do it while I stare at them for five minutes, I write my own stuff down too. It often helps me uncover what is bugging me at certain points in my life and it encourages my clients as well.

Exercise – First Money Experiences

Our first experience of anything new can be really informative when we are looking at our current behaviours. Think back to the first time you remember having any money of your own. How did you receive it? Were you given pocket money given to you, or did you earn it somehow? What did you do with the money? Spend it, save it, or give it away? Did you have complete power over what you did with that money? Write down as much detail as you can about how you felt, what you saw, what you bought and what you did.

Have a quick look back at your written story. How do you feel now about that young person experiencing money for the first time? Are you critical of what they did, or do you understand why that little human acted the way they did? Are there any parallels with your behaviour today and with that younger version of you?

If you find this exercise particularly painful, turn to the extra exercises at the back of the book and do the Money Inner Child visualisation.

A final, helpful word from Jenny.

"I was not very keen to talk about my past, I just wanted to make the future better with my fiancé. Especially when it comes to kids, career and where we will live. But strangely, now I've been able to talk about the past with him, it's

*made talking about the future and what we want for our
lives together much easier. It's been emotional, and I cried
quite a bit, but talking about our money stories helped us
clarify what's important to us. It's like the fog has lifted
and we can see the future paths that we can take together.
To be honest, I don't want my parents' divorce to hang like
a black cloud over our marriage. Now it's been looked at,
I can put it away. I don't feel it has so much power over
me now."*

LOOK BACK AT YOUR Money Pizza Exercise from Chapter
1. Can you see which parts are most influenced
by your money story? For Jenny, she could see how it
affected her Outgoings and Investments, as well as Taking
Accountability for her actions – especially when she tried
to talk about money with her partner.

I invite you – right now - to start a money conversation with
a trusted friend, relative or colleague. Share with them
what you have learned about yourself in completing the
exercises in this chapter. Ask them to tell you their money
story if they are comfortable.

And, voila! The conversation has started.

Chapter Three

Your Money Compass

"When your values are clear to you, making decisions becomes easier."

Roy E. Disney

W HEN YOU IDENTIFY YOUR values and uncover your beliefs about money you can see if your values (how you want to live your life) and your unconscious beliefs (which influence how you actually live your life) point in the same direction. Much of our self-sabotaging behaviour can be traced back to these gaps, as well as your subconscious beliefs, which are the beliefs that linger under the surface of your awareness. It can sometimes be disheartening to realise what they are.

But fear not! I talk with clients all the time about their beliefs and I am constantly examining my own. Believe me, there is always something new to discover about ourselves and more work to do. The key to staying sane is to remember to be kind to yourself. Nobody is born with perfect money habits and beliefs. Nobody.

The link between living according to our values and changing our behaviour to lead a more fulfilling life is so apparent it is often discounted. Honouring our values is essentially fulfilling, even when it is hard to do. In clarifying your values, you can uncover what is truly essential in your life. This will enable you to cut out the crap and make choices based on what is truly important to you. When we do not live according to our values, we feel tense and have a feeling that 'something's not right'. Or, as I like to put it – NQR[1].

Like Your Money Story in Chapter 2, understanding Your Money Compass will relate to all aspects of the Money Pizza. Knowing and understanding your beliefs and values around money is empowering in many areas of your life, including: goal setting; decision making; reining in your spending; and your investment decisions. In fact, beliefs and values are essential in Chapter 4: Money Dramas; Chapter 5: Fearless Financial Review; Chapter 6: Great Financial Decisions; and Chapter 11: Strategic

---

1. NQR = Not Quite Right. When I was growing up, there was an Australian discount supermarket called NQR, which sold products with dents in the tins, damaged packaging and products near their sell-by date. It was daggy, but I miss it.

Investments. Therefore, it is definitely worth spending time understanding them now.

Beliefs and values

Beliefs about yourself tend to be fairly constant (unless you work on them), but values can change depending on where you are in life. You may have valued freedom and flexibility when you were younger, but you might now value stability and security more. Clarifying your values is essential for making good life decisions that will continue to be beneficial for you – and also to help you understand your past behaviour.

Being clear about your values is the key for setting goals you can stick to and work towards. It is important in anything you do to think 'Why is this important to me?' Values help answer that critical question.

If this all seems like fluff, it isn't. Psychologists understand that sometimes unwanted behaviours can be linked back to automatic thoughts and mistaken beliefs. This is at the core of Cognitive Behavioural Psychology, a specialist area of study which seeks to test people's assumed beliefs in order to change knock-on behaviours which may be causing them distress. A key to this area of psychology is the recognition that we are all susceptible to thinking traps like all-or-nothing thinking, catastrophising, predicting the future (and treating it as truth) and mind-reading, for example.

Being able to identify your values can be powerful for changing unwanted behaviours. So powerful in fact, that the most successful rehabilitation programs for people with addictive behaviours tap into the individual's values to help them change. This gentle but powerful technique is called Motivational Interviewing. It encourages people to identify their values, look at their behaviours and – in their own words – examine the gaps between their destructive behaviour and their values.

The pioneers of Motivational Interviewing – William Miller and Stephen Rollnick – recognised that people with addictive behaviours knew their behaviour was doing them harm. Telling people the facts of the damage they were doing to their bodies, bank accounts, brains, relationships and lives made no difference. These people were experts in understanding their lives and they saw what was happening. Brow-beating addicts and drink-driving offenders does no good and has no impact, even worse, it dehumanises them. But when people talk about their values, wishes, and desires, there is space for them to own the decisions around changing their behaviour.

Uncover your beliefs about yourself

Let me share a personal example of how beliefs and values may, or may not, line up. For example, think about the following phrase:

> *"Every person on Earth is trying to balance their beliefs and values. Every person finds it hard work."*

It's a nice thought, isn't it? We are all imperfect beings in the same boat together, trying to improve ourselves. I believe it is entirely true when I am talking to clients and other people. I believe it about everyone, except of course myself. When it comes to me, I don't think it's true. Not really. I want to believe it's true because I value equality and recognising people's common humanity, but when I apply it to myself something is definitely NQR. My inner critic is in my head yelling at me:

> *"You should be better at this! Hell, you are writing a book about it, lady! Who are you to talk about your beliefs, you can't admit to your own?! I'm sure there is someone out there who is better at living a life aligned with their values. Maybe they can write this section. That's right, go out and find someone else – work with an expert. Find someone who is good at this shit. You're never going to make it, so why try? And why write about it either, if you can't get it right..."*

On and on it goes. Even deeper is the thought that someone else would be better at this – it hangs around like a fog. I have the impression that there is a hierarchy of self-alignment – and I see myself standing in a line of people. The people in front of me are better than me, and the ones behind me are worse than me. The line ahead stretches out forever, but I know there is someone who is at the head of the line. Someone else who is the best and the worthiest, and it certainly is not me.

When I sit with this image and think about it – I realise that there is some sort of ideal of perfection swimming around in my head. But I can't define it, I can't put my finger on it. It's just there. At my core I believe that someone must be perfect at this, someone is perfect at aligning their values and core beliefs and they live a perfect life. They are so much better than me and they should be writing this chapter. At that moment, thankfully my conscious brain kicks in and declares: *"What bollocks! You're talking about enlightenment. Whoever has achieved perfect enlightenment? Not even the most enlightened people claim they are perfectly enlightened. Seriously, you have screwed up thoughts, sometimes. But I still love you and I'm glad I'm in your head. Are you actually going to write those swear words? Juicy!"* [2]

---

2. If you think that there is a Zaphod Beeblebrox-type conversational battle going on in my head all the time – you would be right.

This example demonstrates how deeply your beliefs might be hiding. You can see how undermining a negative belief can be. It is not a simple matter of saying "Hey, I see you! Now fuck off!" It takes work and you may have to tackle these undermining beliefs about the perfect way of doing something. You may find once you have attacked one undermining belief, another pops up – so it is an on-going effort.

Sniff out your negative beliefs

Does your self-talk pass the sniff test? By this, I mean, do you start off with something which sounds positive but somehow it doesn't settle as a positive thing for you? The example above starts off as an apparently positive 'we are all in it together' but with a negative undertone of 'actually, it's a bit of a competition and I'm losing'.

You can recognise the sour tone of the negative belief and sometimes that is the only clue you need. It's the feeling that your stated belief doesn't quite tell the full story of you. The negative belief doesn't have to be rational – although it might sound like it is a statement of fact. Trust your gut feeling when something isn't quite right and look a little deeper.

One way of spotting a negative belief is to identify occasions when you extend empathy and compassion to other people in a challenging situation but not to yourself. You somehow hold yourself to an unattainable ideal, but would never do the same for another person. Coaches are exceptionally good at holding this double standard. We can extend empathy to others struggling with their own shortcomings and be silently, brutally, critical of ourselves. Nobody is perfect at this.

When you dig down into it and hear a voice saying "You're never going to make it," this is perfectionism in disguise. It is the idea there is a standard, a model way of being which is so far away from you that you may as well not even try. This can trip you up in many different ways. For example, a client – let's call her Chloe – explained she had initially met a financial advisor 15 years ago who had told her, "You need a Cash Buffer of one year's income". It was such a huge amount, so she gave up right there and didn't do anything about her finances again until we spoke. In retrospect, she realised she had missed many opportunities to build any Cash Buffer because she didn't believe it was achievable.

This belief of: "I'm never going to make it" is often framed by big numbers, massive goals, perfect ideals and arbitrary amounts which are based on undefined standards. It is one of the root causes of procrastination and the easiest way to prevent you from starting something new.

Let me put it another way – imagine you have never run more than 50 metres before and you want to find someone to help you start running. You talk to two potential running partners.

Partner 1 declares: *"You're not a runner until you can do 10km in under one hour. I train at 6pm after work, join me if you want."* [3]

Partner 2 says: *"It's hard work, but if you can improve your fitness until you can run/walk for, say, 1km you will see great benefits already. You might want to continue to do more afterwards, but how about we give that a try? I normally run after work. Would you like to join me for the start of my session?"*

Who are you going to believe, Partner 1 "Real runners are fast'" or Partner 2 "Anyone can try running"? Who is more likely to get you started?

I invite you to think about what this example might highlight about your own beliefs and perfectionism.

When you find yourself thinking, "This doesn't work for people like me" that statement is another way of separating yourself from the pack. Somehow you are different to the majority, or you see someone doing what

---

3. Yes, this is actually something I heard someone say to a beginner runner. I've also heard other clangers like "It's not actually running a marathon if you take walking breaks". I've been running marathons for more than 20 years now, and I can report the people who made these high-standard statements are no longer running. At all. Perfectionism at its worst.

you want to do and think that they are an exception. Who is the exception? You, or them?

We each have different opportunities and setbacks in our lives and upbringing. There are social injustices and inequalities that are real and endemic in our societies. But at the same time, there are elements of our lives where we have true agency and we can take advantage of those. So long as our beliefs are not holding us back.

When we look at people who are famous, recognised experts, intelligent and seemingly successful, we compare ourselves with them and create distance between us and them. The successful ones are more glamorous, wittier, more polished, happier and generally possessing the right genes (while you got the duds). The flip-side of these thoughts is that you are not glamorous, witty, polished or happy enough to be a success in anything.

The problem with beliefs

We like to think we live by our values but really, we are ruled by our beliefs. They are automatic, subconscious and they run around in disguise as ideas that might keep you safe from taking risks and failing. These beliefs also hold you back from pursuing opportunities and making small changes to improve your money situation.

Our beliefs are often passed down by our families, loved ones and – yes – spiritual upbringings. Identifying and separating yourself from these beliefs can be difficult and uncomfortable. It may mean you need to separate your core beliefs from those which your loved ones hold. It can be painful to realise you don't see eye-to-eye on everything. It may also mean you actively look at the social norms which you have been raised to believe are how the world works. That scrutiny takes brave inner work. It is the reading-between-the-lines needed to understand the world. Unacknowledged beliefs have the power to control you without your realising it. They weigh you down and hold you back, so perhaps it's time to let them go.

On the other hand, values are concepts which we actively choose. Values are rarely negative. The notion is that when we live and behave according to our values, we feel more fulfilled and at peace with ourselves. Living in line with our values gives us the inner strength to take risks. For example, when we speak up to defend marginalised people, or when we quit a well-paid job with an unscrupulous company.

People tend to judge their values as either good or bad, and identify values they think they 'should' have. You might feel that spirituality or integrity are better values than personal recognition. However, to understand yourself and your behaviours, suspend this judgement and be true to yourself, especially when you complete the exercises at the end of this chapter. It is rare that you will actively choose a value which is negative or which holds you back. Much that is considered negative is labelled as such by social and cultural norms. Imagine, someone who states they value financial reward. How does that make you feel? Do you think they shouldn't value financial reward?

Peter's beliefs and values story

I discussed this dilemma with a friend, Peter (40) who has a strong Christian faith.

At first, we disagreed intensely about whether or not valuing financial reward was good or bad. I asked Peter a number of questions about why he thought valuing financial reward was bad and morally wrong. He explained that the Scriptures say it is: "'Far better to give than it is to receive" and offered a few more examples of how pursuing wealth was considered a negative belief in his Christian upbringing.

Next, I asked him to put himself in the shoes of a single parent who is considering a choice between two new jobs. One is within the charity sector and the other in the private sector. The parent decides to take the private sector role purely because it pays more. Without knowing anything other than that they are a single parent, is it a negative that this person values financial reward above more altruistic considerations?

This question alone was enough for Peter to recognise his view on financial reward was a belief, not a value.

In this context, he realised someone from a different economic background than him might be held back from providing financial security for their family if they believed financial reward was bad. He also understood this attitude towards financial reward could hold back women more than men because women are far more likely to be single parents. For Peter, the negative view of valuing financial reward was a belief and one that had the potential to disadvantage someone in different circumstances. While he did not have to value financial reward himself, he understood better how our upbringing can influence what we feel are universally positive or negative values.

Weeks later, Peter and I were having another conversation when he reminded me about our robust discussion. He grasped that his own beliefs had the potential to hold his two university-aged daughters back from seeking out well-paid work. He completed the Desert Island Values exercise (at the end of this chapter) and invited his daughters to do it as well.

"I didn't realise how financially insecure they were feeling and I guess that's a difference between us. They both put emphasis on financial reward and being financially stable as something they value. I now don't see that as a negative. I understand they are taking on the responsibility of potentially providing for their future families. I realised how much of myself I was imposing on them."

Peter went on to explain something unexpected that happened next.

"When I looked at my values, I listed openness and trust as something I wanted to live by. But I hadn't spoken with my children about inheritance. I have been doing all the work behind the scenes and I hadn't actually told them about what I had planned. Now that I am talking to them about my plans (acting with trust and openness), it has made the decisions about how to structure the inheritance much easier. I didn't think the conversations would be easy but surprisingly they are, because we can all refer back to our Desert Island Values Exercise as to why we want something a certain way. We don't always agree, but at least we know why, and that makes it easier to resolve."

Peter's original idea that he would not need to talk to his daughters about his inheritance planning is more common than you think. A survey completed in late 2022 by Charles Stanley Direct (an online trading platform) found 14 per cent of high-net-worth individuals in the survey planned never to talk about their inheritance plans with their children! And yet, they were worried about how to preserve the wealth as they passed it down to younger generations.

Value versus values

The human brain loves to take a shortcut whenever it can. If there is an easy way to think about something versus a hard way to think about it, the brain will automatically choose the easy way.

And so it goes for the idea of value, which is the notion that somehow, we can weigh up a cost and benefit and, from that, work out the true price or advantage of something. This usually boils down to a simple little number, with a currency symbol in front, or a percentage sign following.

On the other hand, values are intangible and are hard to compare and contrast. Money is not a value – it is a resource and medium of exchange. Money may, in fact, help you honour your values (such as fun, peace of mind, service to others). But it is the values (not the monetary value) that help determine the rightness of your choices and will help you immensely when you are making financial decisions.

For example, imagine that you are buying a coat. You have found two possible coats to buy – one is £150 and the other is £15. It seems like one is far better value than the other – measured by the number. But consider that the £150 coat is made from local products, employing people on a decent wage, using materials which are produced with a minimum of environmental impact. Sounds good right? But it's expensive and out of the reach of many people on an average salary.

If all coats were produced this way and cost this much, many people would go cold during winter. The other less-expensive coat is imported, made by people in a factory in Far East Asia, living on a subsistence wage. The materials are chemically treated, which makes them cheaper to produce and cheaper to sell. The price tag reflects this and makes a good quality coat available at a lower price for people who don't have £150 to spend on one item of clothing. This is not a bad coat and it keeps its owner warm through winter.

However, the coat you choose will reflect your values, rather than the value of the coat itself.

Have a think about which coat you would prefer to purchase. I invite you to take notes when you consider the following questions.

- Why did you choose that coat?

- Do you always follow this purchasing method?

- Why not?

- Are you making any judgements about someone who would consider the other coat?

- What does that tell you?

The shortcut your brain wants to take is to compare the coats purely on price (or value). You may automatically think that more money means higher quality, or vice versa, but decisions are rarely that easy. Taking the mental short cut may mean that you end up with a coat you can't afford, or one that has a larger carbon impact than you would prefer. A poor decision is more likely. Conversely, making the harder choice based on your values, which takes more cognitive load means that you are less likely to experience buyer's remorse, regret your decision, or feel guilty about a purchase.

Why identifying your values is so important

When you clarify your values, you uncover what is truly essential in your life, enabling you to block out the noise and make choices based on what you find genuinely fulfilling. Your values are the umbrella under which you can make clear-sighted financial decisions.

When you have diverse roles to play in your life, for example, as a manager; student; parent; family member; community volunteer; worker etc, you can feel the pressure of all these roles pulling you in many different directions. This makes decision making and planning almost impossible. I encourage you to think about yourself – instead of one person – as a team of different people (roles) living in the same body. This sounds a bit loopy I know, but it can have a profound effect on how you make decisions. You are not only one consistent whole, but an entire complex system.

You can hear this same idea in many motivational talks – even the internal pep talks you might give yourself. For example, when I'm having a moan about the state of the world, I identify with the angsty teenage me. I embody the grumpy demeanour. I make cutting and pessimistic remarks, and I become as emo as I have ever managed to be. Then a metaphorical light turns on and the grown-up part of me walks into the spotlight in my head and tells me to put on my big girl trousers and get on with life. You can imagine these different roles and characters walking through my brain – each with different costumes and behaviours. It's the Team of Me and I understand how to make all these characters work together. If you would like to look at your Team, flick to the back of the book where I've put some extra exercises.

Coaches working with sporting teams report that discussing and agreeing about people's values is powerful for enabling them to move beyond wall-mounted slogans and straplines. Stated values create a shorthand language for success and great coaches sit down at the start of the season with each of the team members to have the discussion about team values. So, if it can work for sporting teams, why not for the various roles that we take on in our lives?

Values are the way in which we align the different demands that are put on our lives and help us prioritise and make decisions. This is especially important for our financial decisions because we use money to deal with many different issues in our lives.

When our values are well defined and easy to remember, it is easier to recall them when we are making these decisions. You may notice all of the exercises in this chapter are emotive. That is, they will prompt you to feel strong emotions and you may have memorable mental pictures which you can recall, even if you can't exactly remember the words you have used.

As you read on, you may want to come back to this chapter to refresh your memory, or re-do these exercises if you find you have experienced a shift in how you make decisions. This is absolutely normal! You are not a static entity and each shift signals that you have learned something new.

I trust you will realise how profound digging deeper into your own perceptions and beliefs and spending time on yourself can be. This is time well spent and I encourage you to take it slowly. The more clarity you achieve, the easier complex decisions will become. Dilemmas will not have the power to derail you because you will be able to prioritise what is most important in your life right now. Regret about poor decisions will be minimised because you will understand what is driving you and what has served you well before. Behaviour change will be made easier because the invisible hand-cuffs holding you down will be made visible and you might even find the key to unlock them.

Enjoy the journey, this is what life-long learning is all about.

Exercise – Test Your Beliefs

Once you have uncovered a belief, it can sometimes help to test it. Consider yourself a curious scientist. Perhaps you have developed a new theory (uncovered a belief) and you want to see if it works all the time. With your imaginary goggles and lab coat on, you put the theory/belief under the microscope. Use this question sequence below as a guide to examining your belief.

1. What is the theory/belief?

2. What is the evidence that this is true? Do you have proof?

3. Could any of this evidence be faulty? Would it stand up in a court of law?

4. Are there any exceptions to this belief? List as many as you can.

5. Is the belief a fairytale? Impossible? A difficult standard to reach?

6. Is there any evidence that the belief is not true?

7. What would you prefer to believe?

For example, let's revisit Chloe and her unfortunate experience with the financial advisor. As well as the idea that she would never make it, she had other beliefs lying underneath. A key one was "The advisor knows much more than me. I know nothing". We worked through the exercise prompts together and you can read her responses below.

What is the theory/belief?
Chloe's words: "This financial advisor knows so much more about finance, he must be right. I know nothing."

What is the evidence that this is true? Do you have proof?
- The financial advisor is qualified. He has the letters after his name.

- The financial advisor is older than me. He will have more experience.

- The financial advisor is richer than me. He dresses well and has a nice office.

- The financial advisor certainly knows more about numbers than me.

Could any of this evidence be faulty? Would it stand up in a court of law?

- The financial advisor has passed his qualification exams, which is a good thing. But I don't think he understands me well.

- I know other people who are older than me, who aren't necessarily wiser!

- I guess the letters after his name could be fake. But I don't think so.

- I haven't seen the financial advisor's bank account and I guess I never will. The office and the clothes are signals that he might be wealthy – but I'll never really know.

Are there any exceptions to this belief?

- I don't actually know nothing. I have a university degree and I have managed my own money for a number of years.

- I am not in debt. I spend within my means. I know enough to manage my money well enough right now.

List as many exceptions to the rule as you can below.

- He might be an expert in finance, but I am the expert in my life.

- I am an experienced IT technophile. I know how to programme in three different computer languages. I can manipulate statistical data so it is displayed pleasingly. I am an expert in that. I know something (quite a lot actually).

Is the belief a fairytale? Impossible? A difficult standard to reach?

I would call the belief a fairytale. It's like we are playing different characters or archetypes. He knows everything, I know nothing. It's black and white but actually, in reality it isn't.

Is there any evidence that the belief is not true?

- When I was a student, I lived on much less than I do right now and I managed my money really closely. I also knew where to get all the discounts available and how to enjoy myself frugally. I guess I know some things about money – just not what I'd call finance.

- I guess, if I really investigated, there are things about finance that he doesn't understand. Actually, he said something like "Crypto? Don't ask me about that". Maybe he doesn't know everything there is to know.

- When I mentioned how much I earn, he made a

comment which made me think that he would
find it hard to manage with an income like
mine. Maybe he doesn't control his spending
as well as I do.

What would you prefer to believe?
Chloe's words: "This person says he is an expert but
he is not an expert in me and my life. I have a lot of
other skills, including managing my money. I can learn
more".

Exercise – Desert Island Values

Have you heard that radio show called Desert Island
Discs? It's been running on the BBC since 1942 and each
week a guest, called a 'castaway' is asked to choose
a limited number of recordings, a book and a luxury
item that they would choose to bring if they were ever
marooned on a desert island. This exercise is a bit like
that – I invite you to whittle down your values to the key
essential ones.

Read the list of possible values below (deep breath, it's
long). If you think there are any missing, add in your
own. Give each value a score of 1-7 (one meaning not
important at all and seven being extremely important).
Pick the values with the highest score (above 5) and list
them.

From this narrower collection, decide what your five priority values are. Consider these to be the only five values you can take to a strange unknown place – your desert island – and let go of everything else for now.

With these five values in mind, consider – on a scale of 1-7 – are you honouring them in how you behave with money (earning, spending and investing)?

What is the price you pay for not honouring that value?

What is stopping you from living that value?

1. Accomplishment

2. Accuracy

3. Achieve significant things

4. Acknowledgement

5. Adventure

6. Aesthetics

7. Appreciated at work

8. Ascend the corporate career ladder

9. Beauty

10. Being physically active

11. Care for the environment

12. Caring for other people

13. Change and variety

14. Collaboration

15. Community

16. Competition

17. Comradeship

18. Connectedness

19. Creativity

20. Elegance

21. Empowerment

22. Ethical working

23. Excellence

24. Expert status

25. Family friendly

26. Financial reward

27. Flexible working

28. Free spirit

29. Freedom to choose

30. Full self-expression

31. Fun

32. Growth

33. Harmony

34. High performance

35. Honesty

36. Humour

37. Identification with the purpose of my work organisation

38. Independence

39. Innovation

40. Integrity

41. Intellectual challenge

42. Joy

43. Lack of pretence

44. Leaving a positive legacy

45. Lightness

46. Living authentically

47. Make a positive difference to society

48. Nurturing

49. Opportunities to travel

50. Orderliness

51. Participation

52. Particular workplace location

53. Partnership

54. Peace

55. Performance

56. Personal development and growth

57. Personal power and influence

58. Pioneering spirit

59. Productivity

60. Recognition

61. Risk taking

62. Romance

63. Security and predictability

64. Sense of belonging

65. Service

66. Social contact with other people

67. Spirituality

68. Strong relationships

69. Success

70. Sustainability

71. To be a catalyst for change

72. To be entrepreneurial

73. To be well liked

74. To become well known

75. Tradition

76. Trust

77. Using creativity and self-expression

78. Using physical skills and abilities

79. Variety and change

80. Vitality

81. Work-life balance

82. Working to live rather than the other way around

83. Zest

If you are interested in delving a little deeper into your beliefs and values, there are a couple more exercises at the end of the book which you can try.

You now have some powerful tools to change your behaviour. Unhelpful beliefs can hold you back and may need to be addressed. Our beliefs become our thoughts, and our thoughts become our automatic actions so sometimes we need to address those beliefs. The antidote to this is a well-stated set of values. This can help you change your behaviour to align with how you want to live your life.

N ow you have more clarity about your values, you can put that knowledge to good use in any decision that you find yourself making. From buying a coffee in a takeaway cup, to choosing the type of company in which you want to invest your time and your money. Values will bring you clarity.

Life changes = values change = behaviour changes

Look back at your Money Pizza Exercise from Chapter 1. Can you work out in which slices your unhelpful beliefs might be getting in the way? Alternatively, where do your values shine? You may be pleasantly surprised.

It can be easy to forget that as your life changes, so will your values. Values are not set in stone. Twenty years back I valued freedom, hedonism, the latest music and no responsibilities. And, I had a great time living according to those values! Your life will change too – especially when a big transition happens, such as parenthood, unemployment or bereavement. When that occurs, feel free to re-read this chapter and re-do the exercises. You will be surprised how much clarity it gives you.

CHAPTER FOUR

Money Dramas

"If I am not for myself, who will be?
If I am for myself alone, who am I?
If not now, when?
And if not you, who?"

Hillel the Elder c. 10 BCE

S OMETIMES, WE LOOK AT our current dire money situation and cannot find an immediate or easy way out. To make matters complicated, if we identify all the things we can actually do, we might be paralysed by the shame of not having already done those things! It's too uncomfortable to acknowledge that we contribute to (in greater or lesser ways) our own screwed up money situation. That is why it is so much easier to blame someone or something else – but blaming other people will get you nowhere and will fix nothing.

This chapter highlights the most common ways people tend to lay the entire fault about their money situation beyond themselves. Blaming others is a defence mechanism and can keep us feeling safe from responsibility, and ultimately the pain of acknowledging our errors. But the feeling of 'I can't do anything' can keep us stuck. Have a look at where you might be giving your power away (which is what blaming is) to help you choose where and how you want to take responsibility and, ultimately, change your life. Shake off the blame – for other people, for your past mistakes – and take up the opportunity of doing something now. The power to change your life rests with you.

Why we blame other people and the consequences

Like many habits, we pick up the practice of blaming others as we grow up. Blaming something or someone else provides some advantages, it eases painful feelings of guilt, and also allows us to avoid consequences. When we were young, we may have seen other people who used blame to deflect responsibility with seemingly positive results. Or, it may be that having admitted responsibility for something which went wrong, we were made to feel ashamed or punished in some way. We humans have a deep need to see ourselves as better than we actually are and not truly flawed. Making the fault someone else's can help us justify our own actions and avoid the upsetting awareness of our own imperfections.

Blaming others is a defence that helps us avoid recognising and experiencing difficult feelings, such as inadequacy or powerlessness. It's a way we lie to ourselves to maintain our self-esteem, which is terribly important to our sense of self. We use denial of our own responsibility as a way to protect our fragile internal selves from the conflicting demands of the reality we live in – and in some way this helps us function relatively normally.

However, there are many unhelpful consequences of placing the fault of our own situation on others:

1. It stops you from looking at yourself and what you are doing because the focus is on the outside.

2. It prevents you from making positive changes.

3. It adds to a feeling of being powerless and helpless.

4. It robs you of the chance to develop the resilience needed to handle the shit life throws at you.

5. Blaming leads to more blaming. Not only will it become a habit, but it is contagious and will encourage other people around you to do the same and sometimes, blame you!

6. Blaming others will reduce the respect you command and status among your peers.

We know the brain forms and strengthens neural pathways when we practice an action again and again. The repetition embeds these pathways and makes it easier for thoughts and behaviours to slide along them. That is why blaming can become an ingrained habit which is tough to shift.

Think of it like this. Is blaming the best habit you can hold on to, or would you prefer to practice something else? Remember, practice makes permanent. You have a choice to feel like a habitual victim or feel empowered. What will you choose?

Numerous social and psychological studies[1] have demonstrated that if you can minimise the blame placed on external forces and increase the sense of agency and choice that you have for your life, you will build your capability to deal with unforeseen circumstances (especially when they are actually not your fault). I'll say that again. When you stop blaming others for your shit and learn how to deal with it, you will be better able to deal with their shit when they actually do chuck it at you.

---

1. There are too many studies to list, and they are being constantly updated. However, if you are curious to find out more, type 'personal control and external locus' into your favourite search engine and have a look at what pops up.

What do you blame your financial woes on?

Look back to the exercises you completed in Chapter 3: Your Money Compass. Now you have recognised where you may have picked up some of your beliefs, there is a risk of putting the blame of your behaviours somewhere else. Let's have a look at common financial areas of blame.

1 – Your parents (present and absent)

Common themes

"They never taught me how to cope with money."

"They spent everything and now I have nothing."

"If it weren't for their bad habits, I would be wealthy right now."

Antidote

Understand that blaming is a way we protect ourselves – it is a behaviour stemming from the child in each of us and generates powerlessness. Know this: you have a choice now. Even if you think you are young, you are enough of an adult because you are reading this book. Have a little compassion for yourself and your parents. You may want to practice this by using the following phrases as reminders:

- "My parents did the best they could for me, with what they had."

- "My parents did not meet my needs as a child. Now I am old enough I can take care of myself."

- "I have come this far. I know I am strong enough to make positive changes for myself."

- "It's normal to hope that someone will take care of me. I choose to be the person who does."

2 – Your adult children

Common themes

"I spent all this money raising them, it's time I received something back."

"I invested so much time and money in their education, they owe me."

"If they loved me, they would give me money and take care of me."

"S/he still lives at home and it costs so much!"

Antidote

Not too long ago, there was no such thing as savings accounts or retirement planning – having children was the retirement plan! Sometimes money is used as a way to control an adult child – to keep them close to home (either consciously or unconsciously). Or perhaps, having focussed on a child's formal education – and neglecting what might be referred to as life skills – an adult child may not be given the right incentives to seek their own financial independence. Remember, your adult children are not capital investments. It is not a matter of getting a yield or return on investment. They are independent humans – who will strongly resist any form of financial control.

Practise saying the following phrases:

- "I have raised my children and now it is time for me to take care of myself again."

- "I do not need to use money to show love to my children."

- "It is never too late to start taking care of myself financially. I can start today."

3 – Your young children

Common themes

"If I hadn't had a child, I would not be in trouble financially."

"Having a child has destroyed my career."

"It is far too costly to have a child in this country."

Antidote

It may be really difficult to read these sentences – especially if you have young children. These are often deeply-buried beliefs, which we dare not express because they are so taboo. It is socially unacceptable to express regret about having a child and so that regret is transmuted into blaming the cost of raising children.

It is saddening and frustrating – after years of slow progress – to see the global reduction in reproductive rights for women, and the lack of support for families and government support for early education. We should continue to protest these societal injustices. At the same time, we can look to ourselves to be the change we want to see in the world.

Practise saying these sentences too:

- "Raising my children is a financial challenge which I am capable of meeting."

- "My life has completely changed since having a child, and I am making changes as I need to adjust."

- "I am going to be the role model to my children that I never had. I will show them how to be financially resilient."

4 – Society

Common themes

"I was never taught about finance at school."

"Our society is too consumerist and greedy."

"This is just how it is."

Antidote

I encourage you to understand society is in constant flux and evolving – and we influence this change. There may be an impression that change comes from the top, as laws and regulations are updated. But lawmakers and governments only change when there is enough of a popular demand to make laws for fairer societies and improved education. It can feel crushing to imagine you are the only person pushing against the expectations and weight of society.

Seek out other people who are trying to improve their lives and surround yourself with them. You will realise you are not alone and there is support to be enjoyed from people you don't know yet. The following affirmations can help:

- "I may not have been taught about finance at school, so I will educate myself now."

- "I choose to tune into the messages in the media that serve me."

- "I can be the instrument of change that I want to see in the world."

Each person has their own reasons why they are in the situation that they are in right now. Take a bit of time to see where you might be apportioning blame – and be kind to yourself. Instead of trying to change everything, look at the small adjustments you can make.

Do your friends expect you to pick up the bill all the time? Experiment with sitting on your hands when it's time to pay.

Does your partner make all the financial decisions? Have conversations about how you can take responsibility for some of the financial load.

Have you had a costly relationship break up? Tune into a time when you had fewer resources and reconnect with that inventive, younger version of you who found the right solutions in the past.

Recognise financial abuse

It is important that we can also recognise financial abuse when it is happening to us or people around us. Financial abuse – or financial coercion - is a form of abuse which often goes unnoticed and unrecognised. About one in five people have experienced financial abuse – where control of their finances has been taken over by someone else without their consent. Abusers will often gaslight victims so they feel like they are the one responsible for the abuse – or that the victim themselves is paranoid and unstable. Abusers are skilful at making victims blame themselves for their financial situation. Financial abuse is often committed alongside emotional and/or domestic abuse, forming a pattern of bullying and intimidating control.

Signs of financial abuse include the following:

- Being told how to spend your money, or being prevented from spending it.

- Being forced or coerced to give up work and becoming dependent on your partner.

- Being prevented from going to college or university.

- Having to disclose your log-in details, bank cards or Personal Identification Numbers for your accounts.

- Someone spending money that has been allocated for bills and necessities without your permission.

- Someone insisting on managing your money, by transferring assets into their name, and perhaps keeping debts and bills in your name.

- Being forced to constantly ask for money, or an allowance, and made to justify every purchase.

- Being denied access to a partner's financial information, like joint bank accounts or credit cards.

- Withholding of child maintenance payments.

If you, or someone you love, is being financially abused it is best to seek specialist advice and support for the situation. There are helpful UK resources listed at the end of this chapter.

Taking responsibility – Cecilia's money story

Cecilia (32) is an insurance broker in the UK.

"My husband and I bought an apartment in London in 2018. We were both on the mortgage, but agreed to make payments relative to our incomes. I paid 25 per cent and he owned 75 per cent. That meant that I was able to save £8,000 over several years. Unfortunately, my father was ill last year and I had to return to Italy. When he passed away, I stayed in Italy for another nine months to help my mother settle his estate and my savings dwindled to almost nothing.

"When I returned to London and went back to part-time work, my husband separated from me and we will probably get a divorce. While we are still on good terms, it's very painful. And this whole situation is too much emotionally for me. I have no savings anymore, I'm not paying anything into a retirement fund, and I am concerned about what my financial future looks like without the help of a partner. My costs are higher living alone, and I have had to adjust to significantly different spending patterns. That has been particularly painful – I feel like I'm surviving on a shoestring.

"There's so much that has gone on and I feel like all of this stuff is happening to me. It feels really unfair, but I've realised that if I just sit here thinking that it's all really unfair nothing is going to change. Or, it is only going to get worse. I can't turn back the clock – my dad is gone and I don't regret spending that time with my mum. I'm splitting with my husband and there's a fair amount of regret and anger for all the things I could have done to save more money. But I can't change the past.

"So, I have decided to make a couple of changes now. I am about to sign onto a new job – so I will check the salary sacrifice and pension top ups which my new employer offers. If I can't get access to a top up now, I am going to use it as part of my salary negotiation in the future. And yes, I'm going to ask for pay rises on a regular basis – I've never done that before. This will start my retirement pot.

"I have already started to reach out to people to seek financial information and I will probably rely on recently published books by women to get up to speed. That way there is some accountability about the information – rather than following social media accounts.

"Just starting to talk to people about my money situation has made a big difference for me. I know I need to restart saving a Cash Buffer so I have available cash for emergencies. I will make tweaks to my budget in a way that works for me. Once the Cash Buffer and budgeting are reasonably settled, I'll start investing. I think my retirement pot will sort itself out if I can ramp up my contributions, and I am confident I will be able to avoid bad debt."

Can you see the many different opportunities for blame that Cecilia avoids? She shows extraordinary resilience – but probably doesn't recognise it in herself. In taking responsibility for her actions now and simply starting to ask herself important questions, she has developed her own plan to build her financial strength. The change in language is tangible. Towards the end of her story you can feel the momentum and the movement, which is sparked at the point where she decides to make changes herself.

Money roles

You may notice you play different roles in your life – and the same can be said for money responsibility. Be aware of the different roles you play – you may be the responsible leader at work, but when you go out for a drink with friends you switch into a frivolous mode. You may be conscientious when it comes to spending money on household necessities, but rely on other people to provide you with housing or entertainment. It is normal to play these different roles, and being aware of them can provide you with clues about where you might be switching from being responsible to irresponsible.

Have a think about the people around you. What role do you play when you are with your work colleagues, friends, parents, your partner and/or children? What do you say in each situation? What role do you step into and what are the triggers for that change? Do you feel like a child when you discuss money with your partner, but take a leadership role when you are with your friends? What does that tell you about yourself? Complete the exercise below to help change your perspective.

Exercise – Reduce Your Money Blame

Use the following steps to reduce any money blame you may be tempted to hide behind. This also works really well for other types of avoiding responsibility. Take it slowly, and look at each situation, one at a time.

Step 1 – Recognise the blame when it occurs. What is the situation? Who or what is the target of the blame?

Step 2 – Consider the function that assigning blame fulfils for you. Does it help you avoid uncomfortable feelings? Even fleeting ones which flash by? If so, what are those feelings? Write them down, if that helps.

Step 3 – Recognise that being human means making mistakes, having flaws and weaknesses. Take three deep breaths and say to yourself, 'I am an extraordinary, perfectly imperfect human.'

Step 4 – Look closely at how widely you cast your blame. Does it go to your family, your community, your society? The country? The government? The world?

Step 5 – Bring your focus back to yourself and be curious. How might you be contributing to your suffering?

Step 6 – Identify what you could do to address your financial suffering. Write it down, if it helps – or discuss it with a trusted friend.

Step 7 – Understand you do not have to be right or perfect. You do not have to have the perfect plan and you can ask for help. A small step in a positive direction is enough to spark a change.

G O BACK TO THE Money Pizza in Chapter 1 and have
a quick look at your response to the slice I Take
Accountability For My Actions. Do you have more clarity
about why you answered the way you did? How often
are you taking an active role in your financial behaviours?
Draw on those times where you have shown strength,
independence and resilience with your finances and
consider how you can bring more of that brilliance into
your life.

Congratulations to you – the brave soul who has read this
chapter and reflected on your past behaviour. You are on
the path to changing the way you act and the role you play
in your own life.

Resources to assist those suffering financial abuse

These organisations provide support in the UK. If you are elsewhere, search for 'financial abuse support' or 'economic abuse support' in your local area.

Refuge - for women and children survivors of domestic abuse:

https://www.refuge.org.uk/get-help-now/support-for-women/financial-abuse/

Respect – Men's Advice Line:

https://mensadviceline.org.uk/male-victims/what-is-domestic-abuse/financial-and-economic-abuse/

Age UK:

https://www.ageuk.org.uk/information-advice/health-wellbeing/relationships-family/protection-from-abuse/financial-abuse/

Ann Craft Trust – supporting disabled children and adults at risk:

https://www.anncrafttrust.org/what-is-financial-abuse/

CHAPTER FIVE

Fearless Financial Review

*"I learned that courage was not the absence
of fear, but the triumph over it. The brave
man is not he who does not feel afraid, but
he who conquers that fear."*

Nelson Mandela

T HIS CHAPTER WILL HELP you understand fear, why we feel it and how it serves us. You will also discover how to overcome your apprehension so you can have a good look at your finances. Let's face it, at some point in our lives, we get so uncomfortable about our finances, we simply don't want to look. You can admit it to me, you've probably been avoiding checking your bank balance or savings account. Heck, when I started writing this chapter I realised that I had been avoiding looking at my own finances! For two solid years. Talk about, 'Doctor, heal thyself'. It is totally normal if you have put off checking your money position until now, you are not alone.

Many people procrastinate when it comes to focussing on the state of their finances because they are held back by dread. This fear comes from many different places, and it is helpful to understand more about that fear so we can start to overcome it.

Regardless of your cultural background or upbringing, fear is one of the seven universal emotions experienced by everyone around the world. This view is based on research by Dr Paul Ekman, a psychologist, who started studying facial expressions and body movements in the 1950s. At the time of writing, Dr Ekman is 88 years old and he is still fascinated by these universal emotions which include: anger; disgust; surprise; contempt; sadness; happiness; and fear.

You may also have come across research into micro expressions by Dr Wallace Friesan. These are involuntary facial expressions which only last for a fraction of a second. Many people find they can control their emotions to some extent. But these flashes of facial expression can help you understand someone's true emotional state, including your own. Next time you find yourself on a video call, look closely at peoples' immediate expressions in reaction to a suggestion. What flashes of emotions do you see – even in your own face? Look for wincing, a quick smile, a smirk that lasts for a second and no more. What does that tell you about the true emotions in that call?

The intensity of the fear we experience can range from feeling a bit of trepidation or nervousness, all the way up the scale to panic, horror and terror (with anxiety floating somewhere in between). Usually, we experience fear as a low-level uneasiness or rumble of apprehension. However, when you are faced with the idea of having a look at your financial situation, you may experience fearful emotions bordering on dread, or a heavy physical feeling as if you are being weighed down and are waiting for the end of the world. When you can understand the depths of emotion that these surface level feelings indicate, it is not surprising that split second experiences can derail you from making any advances in tackling your financial situation.

As I write these words in 2024, odds are we are heading into a prolonged and widespread period of global anxiety, if not recession. Energy costs have risen and inflation has sent living costs through the roof for many people. Add to that the change in global monetary policy, which has seen central banks reverse the decade-long policy of ultra-low interest rates – which means our mortgage rates and housing costs have gone up. Not to mention the climate crisis. Is it any wonder, with all of these changes happening around us – and to us – we are frightened about what the hell might happen next? We might be managing well enough now, but what on earth is around the corner?

Why are we fearful?

It is completely normal to experience fear and anxiety. However, when this fear stops us from acting we start to think fear isn't useful at all. But, what else (other than looking at our money or lack of it) makes us scared and fearful?

The universal trigger for fear is the threat of harm, which could be real or imaginary. It doesn't make a difference to how our body experiences those feelings of dread. A threat could be to our physical, emotional or psychological wellbeing. It is clear that a hazard to our financial wellbeing – such as a potential loss of income or increase in costs – will influence our feelings of safety and security, causing our fear reaction to spike.

It is important to understand that we can learn to become afraid of nearly everything if we do not pay attention. This is what may happen when there is a constant stream of negative bad news around you. When we scroll through social media or news sites, unconsciously looking for more upsetting news (doom-scrolling) it makes us feel worse than when we started – even if we thought we were only trying to stay up-to-date. We use the habit to avoid the slight discomfort of boredom, but it can end up making us feel worse in the long run.

Remember how I said that your body reacts the same way to real or imagined threats? You can think yourself into such chronic anxiety, that the stress put on your heart and your body can damage your cardiovascular system. This is through the effect of constant adrenaline and cortisol (the so-called stress hormones) pumping through your body. These chemicals keep sparking the fight-or-flight reaction, which raises your heart rate, makes you sweat and gives you the jitters. If your body doesn't have a chance to recover, it stays on high alert permanently – with long-term physical effects on your body and general health. This is why it is so important to gently face your fears and overcome that anxiety so you are not constantly under this stress.

Running away from anxiety

We avoid many situations so we don't have to feel anxiety or manage that awkward feeling when we face the unknown. For example, if we walk into an electronics store we might put off asking about a product we don't know much about because we don't like the feeling of looking ignorant. Like anyone else, I feel more comfortable researching online for an hour about a potential purchase, rather than calling a human to ask for their help. We also avoid asking important questions (especially about money) because we are fearful about seeming stupid to someone else. Fear is associated with embarrassment and more than a little bit of shame.

Even mild uneasiness or discomfort holds us back from doing so much in life. We avoid many conversations because we don't like the feeling of awkwardness in our bodies which is evoked by apprehension. We don't like the physiological responses (high heart rate, sweaty palms) when we do something new, or something which we are not used to doing. This is because the brain releases chemicals into our body causing physical feelings which make us uncomfortable.

However, you can choose to spin this experience around so it works better for you. Discomfort is a sign you are learning something new, so you can choose to avoid it (and learn nothing) or embrace the discomfort as part of acquiring a new skill. Easier said than done – but it can help reframe your feelings.

Be fearful or pay attention?

The hormone adrenaline alerts your brain and your body to pay attention. You might be starting something novel and there is a new skill you need to learn. The same physical sensations (which you could interpret as fear) are preparing you to take on new information. Your heart beats faster, so there is more oxygen going to your brain. This ensures you are ready to respond quickly to the new information. These physical feelings might be a little uncomfortable – but you could choose to tell yourself your body is feeling excited rather than fearful or anxious. Fear and excitement often have the same physical cues.

Kimberly Wilson, who presents a fantastic podcast called *Made of Stronger Stuff,* suggests we can change our perception of anxiety to a perception of excitement. The sensations of anxiety signal that your body and brain are marshalling their resources to learn something new. Kimberly recommends reframing those feelings of discomfort and unease in a different way. When you feel anxious the result is often retreat, avoidance and worry. But if you feel pumped, excited and ready to go, you can use these feelings to head towards the problem you are facing.

Kimberly's way of overcoming her feelings of fear is to say to herself: "This is only a sign that my body is preparing me. This is normal. This is my body working perfectly well, preparing me for this new action that I am about to take. Thank you, body. Let's go." This positive self talk can take the edge off the anxiety.

What fear means for your finances

Let's get back to looking at your financial situation. It's important to consider your financial position on a semi-regular basis. I recommend if you have never done this before, now is the time. Think about your finances right now. Open up your bank account and take a look. If you checked your finances before, but it was in the distant past, it is worth revisiting the exercise. Do this at least every year, or so, or after any big life changes, including: starting a family; moving in with someone; a family break up; or a bereavement. Better still, review your finances before you make a big decision.

If you have any strong feelings, such as you tell yourself that you hate the paperwork, I encourage you to recognise this for what it is. It is an excuse to procrastinate, which hides an underlying fear. In fact, there are many people who think procrastination is the brain's way to avoid pain. I say instead, embrace your fear.

Do you hate the paperwork? If so, try thinking of each piece of paper as a stepping stone towards your financial goals. Do you dread looking at your balances and debts? Remember, the numbers are data and information. They point the way to where your focus should be. Take the self judgement away. Your bank balance does not reflect whether or not you are a good person. You are an exceptional person who is making extraordinary improvements. You are fantastic, strong and resilient. Now go and look at your bank balances!

Acknowledge your fear. You might find it useful to speak the words describing your fear out loud. For example, 'I am scared of what my bank balance says about me as a person.' Saying it out loud can have a cathartic effect, creating distance between you and the words, and diffusing the statement. You may feel silly having said it, and that is okay too. You may feel a little shiver as you say it and you could imagine that it is your body letting go of the fear.

It is often said that behind your biggest fear is your biggest success. If you are feeling apprehensive now, imagine there is a big success waiting for you once you step around that worry. I have seen this so often with people taking control of their financial lives, and I also rely on this viewpoint when I feel afraid of facing up to a challenge.

Your quick and dirty financial check up

This is where we talk about how you can complete your quick financial review. You can make it as detailed or as off the cuff as you like. I tend to prefer quick and dirty. I recommend you notice the things you want to avoid. What makes you want to skip 'that thing' that you know you should look at? Is it because of practicalities (e.g. the number is too insignificant to move the dial) or are you avoiding something important?

I like to use four different time buckets, which are labelled: Right Now; This Year; Medium Term (5 Years); and Long Term. You might notice that this goes against the grain of general advice about being as detailed as possible with your finances. Practically speaking, when it comes to making timebounded decisions, this is the maximum your brain can handle.

You may have great savings for retirement, but because you won't be accessing them right now you need to put them into the LongTerm bucket. Or, if you are retired and they are part of your income, this will feature in your Right Now, This Year, and Medium Term bucket. It all depends on your unique situation, and you are the best person to make that judgement. I'll explain more below.

Right Now: What is your income and what are your outgoings, right now? This is current cash flow, in and out of your accounts. It's fine if you are going backwards for now (have a look at Kate's example later). It's good to know what you are spending each month (even if it doesn't look pretty).

This Year: What resources could you use to get your hands on more cash if you need it? This includes your savings and emergency funds but it can also include anything that you can liquidate (sell) to generate cash. This might be clothing, equipment or other possessions that you can sell second hand if you need/want to. In expenses, detail any upcoming costs you want to include. This could be a trip, health care costs, car repairs or house renovations. Again, it's up to you to choose what is relevant for you right now, although I encourage you to check with a trusted friend that you haven't missed anything important.

FINANCIAL CHECK UP

	PART A - INCOME AND ASSETS (THINGS THAT CAN GENERATE FUTURE INCOME)	PART B - EXPENSES AND LIABILITIES (THINGS THAT CAN GENERATE FUTURE EXPENSES)	NET RESULT (PART A MINUS PART B)	SO, WHADDAYA THINK ABOUT THAT?
NOW This month	Income, salary, rental, any other regular(ish) payments	Monthly expenses (An estimate is good enough)	*How are you doing right now?*	
THIS YEAR The next 12 months or so	Cash in the bank; restricted but accessible accounts	Any big expenses coming up (Car repairs, Home repairs, Travel, Events, Health etc)	*What about the near future?*	*Are things looking good, shaky or bad?* *Are these the results you expected to see?*
MEDIUM TERM 1 to 5 years	Investments which can be sold reasonably easily eg shares traded on an exchange	Lease repayments, increase in mortgage costs (after fixed periods end)	*What's the outlook like in the near future?*	*What are the good bits?* *What are the bits that you think you should focus on improving?*
LONG TERM	Investments which can take longer to sell; home; other property; pension/retirement funds	Property Mortgage and other long term loans	*How about further out?*	

Medium Term: This is pretty much the same idea as Right Now, but framing it for 5 years in the future. I tend to put any possible stocks and shares, and other liquid investments in this bucket. It's important to understand that any form of investment should be held for the longer term rather than the shorter term. But life gets in the way sometimes – and you have to sell your investments at some point. Slightly underestimate the value of your assets and slightly overestimate the amount of your expenses that might come up.

Long Term: These are assets or income that you are unable to access for more than 5 years. Finance people like to call these 'illiquid' assets because they are more difficult to sell, or they are literally frozen until you reach a certain time point. For many people, private pension savings will make up the bulk of their Long Term assets. If you have investments in property (either your own home or some sort of rental), put those assets here. Be aware that some investments have a lockup period, meaning that you cannot access your money for a fixed amount of time, or under certain circumstances. Often older people who have a significant amount of equity in their home will notice much of their wealth is parked in this Long Term bucket, but may find that their immediate income and outgoings are mismatched.

The benefit of mapping out your financial situation is that you can tally up the resources which are already available to you, but which you might overlook. When you are completing this financial checkup, it's fine if you know the numbers roughly off the top of your head. Although it is good to confirm your guesses wherever possible by checking your accounts.

Remember, while it may seem like a lot of work, checking account balances now involves either looking up an app on your phone or computer, or pulling out your paperwork from a drawer. It actually doesn't take too long. Do not be tempted to reorganise your life before you check your paperwork. Simply go and find that piece of paper which tells you what you need to know. Reset passwords if you must. Whatever you do, check those accounts.

Kate's check up story

Kate (42) quit her corporate management role in the middle of the coronavirus pandemic to retrain and start a new business.

> *"I couldn't stay in my job; it was killing me. I had asked years ago for flexible working and had been refused. I put a plan in place for me to quit my job and train to do something else. It took years of planning and then the coronavirus pandemic hit and we were locked down for months. I had to reconsider my decision to quit, but I couldn't continue working for that company."*

"I am glad I quit and I didn't don't regret it. But everything took much longer to ramp up than I thought. Also, I caught coronavirus, which knocked me back about six months in my business because I was too exhausted to do anything.

"I have promised my little family a big trip overseas to see our bigger family – and it is really important to all of us. The trip will be rip-roaringly expensive. When travelling with my family, I seem to bleed money. I got a travel agent to lock in prices for us a few months back and that has saved us from some unexpected price rises. In a few months, I need to pay £14,000 and that seems ridiculous when I am not earning anything. But I feel like I can't cancel the trip; for myself or my family. If we don't go, we will miss an important family wedding and seeing a number of new baby cousins. I think it would be such a shame.

"At the same time, I am having anxiety dreams about how we will to lose the house and end up on the streets. My brain is fast-forwarding to me in old age being homeless and it is scary! I know it is irrational but I can't seem to make the practical connection between now and the future. Part of me wants to keep going as I am, without changing anything, and the other part of me is really worried about when the money will run out. I really don't want to look at my money, at all. When I think of 'taking

the temperature' of my financial situation I just want to close my eyes and ignore it.

"It seems like so much paperwork, and I have to chase up bank accounts that I had not managed to close during the pandemic. I tried, but it was such a flipping hassle that I gave up.

"Also, my mortgage is about to roll off its fixed rate and I am not sure what to do. I did my brief sums last week and I worked out that our costs will increase by £500 per month. What am I doing? Am I really going to have to cancel our holiday? I still have my bonus from the old job saved up for it, but I don't know if I am throwing good money after bad."

Kate agreed that it was a good idea to write these things all down on paper so she could see the big picture. You can see Kate's check up on the next page. After doing the quick and dirty financial check-up, Kate said:

"I realise I am bleeding money faster than I had hoped, but not as fast as feared. The Big Trip spending will take a massive chunk, but I still feel like it is worthwhile for a precious opportunity. But what is clear is that between now and the trip, I have to increase my income somehow."

KATE'S FINANCIAL CHECK UP	PART A - INCOME AND ASSETS	PART B - EXPENSES AND LIABILITIES	NET RESULT	KATE'S THOUGHTS AND NOTES
NOW This month	Monthly income £400	Monthly expenses £5,000	-£4,600	Well, I'm going backwards quickly and that's no lie. I really wish I wasn't at this point. I'm going to have to put more effort into increasing the income and reducing the expenses.
THIS YEAR The next 12 months or so	Cash in the bank & Whatever the Fuck fund £37,000 Restricted bank accounts £5,500	The Big December Trip (but paying in October) £14,000	£28,500	#1 - I really need to close those restricted accounts #2 - I have 6 months left at this burn rate (£28,500/£4,600 - 6.2) which takes us to April #3 - This is not going to look good when we are remortgaging in April
MEDIUM TERM 1 to 5 years	ISA stocks and shares £37,000	Mortgage costs expected to go up by £500/month in April —> extra £6,000 outgoing per year	£31,000	I'm OK enough here for a year - but it's not going to be great to liquidate my shares. I really don't want to because I've hear it's about 'time in the market' and I don't like the risk of the prices dropping next year. But if I had to I could.
LONG TERM	Home valuation £720,000 Retirement fund £109,000	Mortgage principal outstanding £323,595	£505,405	Gawd, if you only look at these numbers I'm flipping minted! I took a conservative home value, because I think it's more realistic. But I can't just sell up the home to make more money. In any case, it takes AGES to sell a house and get the cash. At least, this makes me feel better about my long term wealth. So I can focus my efforts on the near term.

"It is not going to be enough to only cut back on expenses but we have to try. When I look at it, we can probably take 10-15 per cent off our expenses if we are careful, but not much more. I have a smaller amount in several overseas accounts that is worth gathering in. If I need a full day's administration to work all this out and wait on a phone, it will be worthwhile.

"I'm relieved to I have six months' cash left at our current spending rate and it seems okay. But I have to remind myself that if I am totally out of cash by then, I will have to start liquidating my stocks and shares, which I really don't want to do. In the end, I can put my stocks towards the mortgage so the money won't disappear completely and won't be wasted. I call that my Plan C. Long term, it looks like I will be fine as long as I return to paying more money into my ISA and savings.

"At the end of the day, I always knew that I needed to increase my income but I had been avoiding the reality. Now this exercise has made it much clearer and given me a timeline to work towards. I am okay for now but the clock is ticking. At least this way, I can park my worries about the trip, the medium term and the long term and get cracking on attracting more clients to my business.

"Fundamentally, my story hasn't changed. It has become more focused. I know what I need to do now. Plan A is to increase my income as quickly as possible. I have ideas

about what to do and I need to put that plan into place immediately.

"Plan B is to talk with my family about reducing our expenses. I find this a much more daunting prospect than getting new clients!

"Plan C I don't really want to do. But if I made it Plan Z or avoided it altogether, that isn't realistic either. Maybe we will say no to any new big-ticket items like travel for now, and consider it more of a Plan D to dip into the stocks and shares if I must. But I really don't like that idea. So that is motivation enough to make sure Plan A and Plan B work."

Your Financial Check Up Exercise

There is only one exercise in this chapter because it is so important. Using the guidance and example above, make yourself comfortable, collect the information you need within arms' reach and fill out your Financial Check Up, using the blank template provided on the next page.

Do this. Right now.

YOUR FINANCIAL CHECK UP

	PART A – INCOME AND ASSETS (THINGS THAT CAN GENERATE FUTURE INCOME)	PART B – EXPENSES AND LIABILITIES (THINGS THAT CAN GENERATE FUTURE EXPENSES)	NET RESULT (PART A MINUS PART B)	SO, WHADDAYA THINK ABOUT THAT?
NOW This month				
THIS YEAR The next 12 months or so				
MEDIUM TERM 1 to 5 years				
LONG TERM				

Amazing! How do you feel now? Is it as bad as you thought? Is there work to do? However you feel about looking at your financial situation right now, understand that you have taken a huge step forward. You have completed your Fearless Financial Review!

W HENEVER YOU FEEL A little lost with your finances, you can now come back to this chapter and grasp a solid anchor, which always shows you where you are.

Have a glance back at the Money Pizza and the slice: I Am Not Afraid To Review My Finances. Chances are you have improved your original evaluation of that slice, now you have completed your review. The key to maintaining this skill is regular practice. If you can arrange a regular day to do it (at least annually) you will come to realise that the results don't matter as much as the practice of doing a regular financial review.

CHAPTER SIX

Great Financial Decisions

*"A wise man makes his own decisions; an
ignorant man follows public opinion."*

Chinese Proverb

D O YOU FIND FINANCIAL decisions terrifying? Confusing?
Complex and convoluted? By the end of this
chapter, you will realise that while tricky at times,
embracing difficult emotions and learning to deal with
ambiguity is all part of making great decisions.

The right decision

This is the Holy Grail of finance – making the best, optimal,
perfect, correct and right-in-all-scenarios decisions. All the
time. And like the Holy Grail – it is mythology. An incredible
story, a magical thing that we can search for, strive for,
and we will never find it.

Soz.

But what about a 'good enough' decision? Or, the best decision for what you have right now?

Would you believe me if I said these are great financial decisions? These are the decisions which embrace complexity, emotion, imperfection, and allow you to take action. I am sorry that no decision will ever be perfect. However, you *can* make great financial decisions.

Sunk costs

I was asked to run a workshop about budgeting for non-financial managers. As part of the workshop, I introduced a few finance definitions so the attendees had the vocabulary to discuss business budgets with their financially-trained peers. I was surprised to find out most people were especially interested in the concept of sunk costs.

A sunk cost happens when you have made a financial decision and cannot recover the cost regardless of the outcome. For example, you buy t-shirts for a branded event in 2020 and had the shirt made, before finding out the event is cancelled. You have spent the money and have all these items, but you can't recover any value from them. These are your sunk costs.

Traditional budgeting says you need to ignore those costs entirely. But it's not that easy because (a) the money is no longer in your budget, and (b) it hurts to admit that.

To put this in context of what this might mean for you, I will use an example from one of the workshop attendees. Irina entered a triathlon scheduled for 2020, spending a hefty €300 on the entry. The event had to be postponed due to various lockdowns and was due to run in 2022. In those two years, Irina's life had changed and so had her fitness level. The costs of flights and accommodation to attend the triathlon had gone up three-fold (so her original budget had been blown completely). Her partner tried to explain that the €300 entry was a sunk cost and she shouldn't be trying to recover that value.

Attending the rescheduled event would cost her more than €2,000 (not including the original entry fee which wouldn't be refunded). But the desire to recover the entry fee (and her fitness) meant Irina kept increasing her financial commitment to the trip.

Sunk costs have a natural pull on us. It's not easy to unhook ourselves from a costly original decision so we can leave it behind and start afresh. While the textbooks suggest we are best to ignore sunk costs entirely, in reality, it is tough to do so.

Firstly, there is the regret of making a poor decision and the desire to put it right. If you dropped €300 on the street and realised it quickly enough, you would retrace your steps to try to find it. But what if you realised that you had left the money in a taxi yesterday – in another country? The mistake hurts like hell, but retracing your steps and recovering the money is much more difficult. It is likely you won't even try (and you might have a bit of a cry which is, of course, okay). The point at which you decide to shrug your shoulders and move on depends on you, how big your loss is and the chances you perceive of recovering the money. This plays out in everyone's decision making process.

If you have a similar experience to Irina, I invite you to reframe the situation so you can start afresh. Instead of having paid for the entry, imagine instead, that you had been offered free entry to a triathlon. Your fitness is not perfect, and expenses to get there are pretty high. On the other hand, it is a triathlon that you would like to do and this is your chance at a free entry. What would you do? Would you make a different decision for a free entry, versus an entry fee you are trying to recover?

The regret of a bad decision

Regret is a powerful emotion that keeps us stuck and hampers our ability to make the best decisions. Behavioural economists call this 'regret aversion bias', which recognises the pain of regret (or loss) is far more powerful than the pleasure of a gain. If you are thinking of a past regret – for example, a poorly considered property purchase – you are likely to be influenced by regret aversion when making future property-related investment decisions. This bias might encourage you to favour an investment decision that reduces the risk of making the same mistake. Or you may unconsciously try to fix the past decision by using the investment decision in front of you.

In some ways, the best way to deal with regret is to recognise it and understand you cannot fix past mistakes. You can only make different decisions now. Be honest about where you might be tied to past decisions when you are making the decisions for today and the future. While it is always a good idea to reflect upon what you could learn from your mistakes, it is important to dial down the self-criticism. The more critical you are of yourself, the more likely you will hold onto the pain of regret and continue to make unhelpful decisions. Dr Julie Smith talks about self-criticism and making mistakes in a powerful way in her book *Why Has Nobody Told Me This Before?*

> *"Those who are highly self-critical are more likely to be critical of others. If we believe that mistakes and shortcomings should be met with humiliation and shame no matter what the intention, how do we ever begin to be okay with taking risks and making mistakes ourselves?"*

How traditional financial theory screws up decision-making

Trustworthy financial advisors and money managers are exceptional professionals. When you work with a great financial advisor, you will know how much of a difference they can make to your wealth and financial confidence.

However, traditional financial advisory can be a source of frustration for clients and practitioners alike because (as the word 'traditional' suggests) the profession has been built on old-fashioned practices. Once upon a time, the business of financial advice was reasonably simple. Clients were usually men, with high incomes, with at-home wives to support their careers and money-making efforts. The financial advisors looked and had lifestyles very much like their clients and the industry was rather homogeneous.

Decision-making for these clients (and advisors) was simplified by one line of employment income (no portfolio careers here!) and reducing the wife and kids to mere cost lines on the money tally. To introduce the wishes and needs of a spouse (often with different life-goals) and children (ditto) into the financial decision making was beyond the scope of the client or advisor. So, these wishes and needs were largely ignored.

A simple scenario, with few variables, can support a simple decision. This gives us the impression that there is a correct or optimal decision to be made. Finance textbooks are written in this way – scenarios are simple, and you can look up the correct answer in the back of the book.

However, today's wealth management client is far more complex. Often, they are female and do not want to compartmentalise their lives in the old-fashioned way. Women - and many men nowadays - are far more tuned into the system in which they live. When making financial decisions, they take into account knock-on effects on their children, parents, peers and the environment. Learning how to deal with such complexity and ambiguity is complicated. Unfortunately, most (not all) financial advisors shut down such conversations. I know financial managers and advisors who take the time to have these conversations but they admit that (a) such conversations are not part of their business strategy; and (b) they have little training in those knotty areas .

The truth is nobody is the expert in your life but you. It is up to you to embrace your decisions in all their complication, and understand that there will be no perfect decision. Does that make you feel uncomfortable? You are not alone. Maybe, it is better to know that there is such a thing as a good enough decision, rather than a perfect decision.

Take it all on yourself?

You might be reading this chapter because you feel you need to step up and start making adult decisions. Perhaps nobody around you is capable of making these decisions and you are taking on the responsibility. I applaud you for stepping into such an important role. However, I also recommend you do not make these decisions in isolation from the people around you. You live within a system of people and relationships, and these have a great influence on your choices, whether you like it or not. People can fall into the trap of not considering those people around them when making financial decisions, because they discount everyone else's financial decision-making abilities.

For example, Manooj (52) was thinking about a property purchase for his family home. He had decided to pursue a property, which was further away from his work, but had more backyard space and allowed the possibility of purchasing a pet. He took his family to see the house and they seemed enthusiastic.

I asked Manooj to go back to his family and have a conversation about whether or not they should actually go ahead with the purchase, before committing to it. He was tasked with sharing all the information that he had, what it would mean in terms of changes in commuting, garden space, needing to earn or save more money as a family – everything. He was sceptical because his partner stayed at home and didn't work, and his children were young (6 and 10 years old). He didn't think they would have anything valuable to add to the conversation. I suggested to Manooj that at the end of the day, the decision was his, but it could be helpful to ask his family for their input about the decision. Manooj was frank with me and said, "I don't normally involve my family in these decisions. This is not how I like to do it." In the end, he could see that it was worth a try.

After taking the time to talk to his family, Manooj said:

"I thought I was doing the right thing by making this decision myself, and shielding my wife and our kids from the choice. It was all too big for them and I feared that it would turn into a conversation where my children made a wish list of all the things they wanted. Instead, we all sat down after lunch one weekend and I shared all the information I had in front of me.

"I told them about how I thought the new place would be good for playing and that we might adopt a dog. I also told them that it would mean I would be home 30 minutes later each evening and would have to leave in the morning before they all woke up. I set out all the pros and cons that I could think of, including needing to pay more money for the mortgage each month.

"It turned into a long conversation. My children asked some extraordinary things which I didn't expect, like, 'if you have to pay more money, will you have to work harder?' And they also told me that they much preferred playing in the park nearby, because it had swings and their friends were often there. They did say that they wanted their own rooms but that they didn't want huge rooms, which surprised me. If it meant having a huge room, or being near their school friends, they wanted to be able to ride to their friends' places, when they were old enough, of course.

"My wife loved the idea of having a bigger kitchen and a separate laundry but wasn't keen on the dog at all. She also pointed out that we would need to have a separate car for her to drop the kids to school, and for her to access any public transport. It turned out that the kids didn't like the idea of actually cleaning up dog poo and I realised that we would be creating another burden to manage. She asked me if we were going to hire a gardener and I laughed for a bit. But she made a good a point. I have never had to mow a lawn before and I am not sure I want to start now.

"Without realising it, I was creating more of a burden financially and also in terms of maintenance time for a house that looked beautiful on paper. My kids were completely uninterested in doing any extra chores and my wife stated plainly that she wasn't interested either. I had

been so set on buying a family home, but I hadn't actually spoken to the family. I feel like I have to go back to the drawing board and start all over again. But it's better than making the wrong decision.

"I can't say it was an easy conversation for me. At times it was frustrating because I didn't feel like they were taking the conversation seriously and I don't think they recognised how much effort I had put into this on their behalf. I was tempted to simply keep going with my decision. But I was forced to wait two days anyway and in that time, I changed my mind. Involving my family in the decision has been time-consuming and frustrating, but in a strange way it has also taken the burden off me to find the perfect home and make the perfect decision."

The best financial decisions are boring

If you are looking for an interesting thing to talk about at your next social event, it should not be your investments or spending patterns. Great investments and financial decisions are boring, they are unsexy and they won't be a great conversation starter. They are lower risk, and do not involve anything involving zeitgeist or amazing wealth creation or whatever BS is being spouted on social media. Great decisions minimise the drama, for yourself and your wallet.

Do you really want to say the following phrases?

"I made so much money on this trade yesterday!"
"This house is AMAZING! It is our forever home."
"And I just said ... hang the cost, we're only going to get married once!"[1]

If so, you are reading the wrong book.

Great financial decisions are boring. They should put your dinner party guests to sleep with their mundanity. Consider this:

"I invest some money every month in a low-fee tracker fund. In fact, I'm not sure how much is in the account – it's modest. I check it once a year."
Yawn.

"We bought this smaller house because it fits well within our budget."
Ho hum.

"We are considering a small event. I don't think you could make a reality TV show out of it."
Oh, my word stop the tedium.

These boring financial decisions are the ones I celebrate! Do you go after the big, flashy, stuff? I hate to say it, but you are following the big-flashy-herd off a big-flashy-financial-cliff. High risks, big spending,

---

1. Incorrect, as Richard Burton and Elizabeth Taylor proved to us all!

overusing debt, these things will make other people wealthy, but not you. This is so important right now when we are dealing with high inflation and market volatility. Do not 'buy the dip' like some crypto bros want you to. Start small. Be consistent. Grow at your own pace. Above all, be supremely comfortable with what you are doing with your money and find your adrenaline rush elsewhere.

Value-based or values-based decisions?

Remember in Chapter 3, when you looked at your values? Flick back right now and refresh your memory. When you are faced with a choice of options – on investments, spending priorities, whatever – and you are dissatisfied with your choices. What do you do? How do you make the least-wrong decision? You may be presented with a choice between something which will make or save you a lot of money or a more expensive alternative. What is better for you? If you find any resistance going for the value-based decision or the rational, economic decision, it may be worth revisiting your values.

What are the values you hold close to your heart? How would you like people to talk about you when you are not around? Is the financial choice in front of you reflective of these values? If not, it is time to consider your alternatives.

Are you making a value-based decision, where you are influenced by the money alone?

Or, are you making values-based decisions, where you consider what more is important to you?

Sometimes choosing one is more difficult than the other. While a values-based decision might be more difficult at first, it is more likely to make you feel fulfilled in the long run.

Putting it differently, which decision will you be proud of making when you look back on this moment in the future? The one you are more proud of is your values-based decision. Tune into this because in the future, it will be the one that gives you comfort when life gets difficult and you question your life choices.

Happy to make financial decisions

As you reflect on your Money Pizza, what strikes you about the slice that asks you to consider if you are happy to make financial decisions? Do you need more time to reflect about what might be holding you back from being comfortable making these decisions, or is this chapter all you need?

Have a look at the rest of the Money Pizza. How has your decision-making affected the other parts? What do you realise you might be doing unconsciously in your spending, debt use, or investments? Are your financial decisions keeping you stuck, or do they allow flexibility?

Have a quick look now, and see what thoughts and ideas come up.

Your Inner Critic Exercise

Tune into how your inner critic could be hijacking your thoughts by taking some time to consider and answer these questions.

1. How do you deal with your own and other people's mistakes? What do you think, and what do you do?

2. When you hear about someone who makes bad financial decisions and ends up in a poor situation, what kind of language do you use to describe them in your own head?

3. Now think about yourself again. How do you deal with your own mistakes and failures? Do you berate yourself? Do you have the urge to fix the mistake or failure in some way? How does this affect you? Do you like this inner voice that talks to you? If you don't like it, how can you reduce the volume?

Disaster Planning Exercise

When considering an investment decision, do you know all the possible things that could go wrong (or right)?

Sometimes, it helps to clarify what these things are, so you can target your efforts on factors within your control.

Using sticky notes or small pieces of paper, give yourself 15 minutes to list all the things that could go wrong with your proposed investment.

Then, get another piece of paper (or use a whiteboard if you have one handy) and draw two crossing arrows, as below.

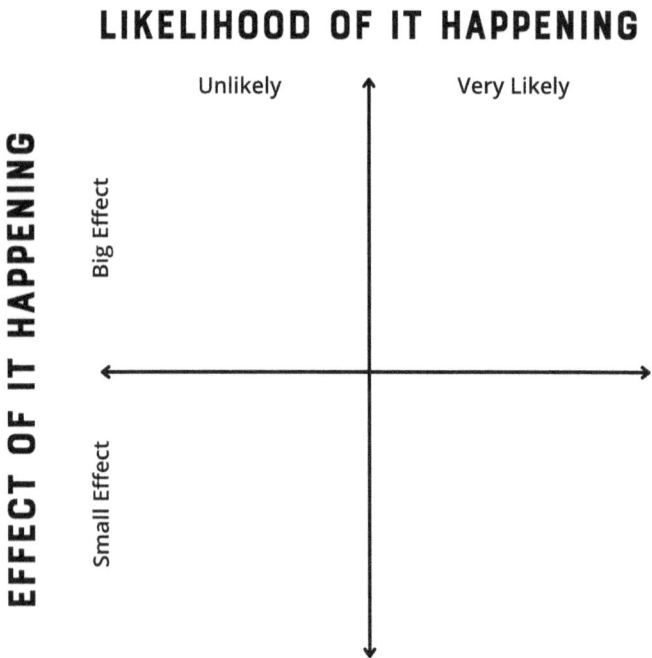

LIKELIHOOD OF IT HAPPENING

Unlikely   Very Likely

EFFECT OF IT HAPPENING

Big Effect

Small Effect

Make sure you consider these important scenarios:

- Being unable to sell when you want to.

- Not getting the right price when you sell.

- The investment takes longer to start paying dividends/rent/income than anticipated.

- The investment never pays an income.

- The investment is damaged in some way.

- The investment requires more time than you expected.

- The investment requires additional funds to be put in to help it grow.

Keep going until you run out of ideas of what could happen.

Now place all the events you wrote down in the appropriate part of the grid. What do you notice? Are all the 'could go wrong' events clustered near the one spot? What does that tell you about the investment you are considering? Are these risks that you can manage yourself?

Look at the following graphic, and consider how big or small your risks are. What concrete, practical and reliable steps can you take to mitigate these risks? Are you satisfied with the information you have, or is there more work to do to understand the decision you will make?

LIKELIHOOD OF IT HAPPENING

Unlikely   Very Likely

EFFECT OF IT HAPPENING

Big Effect

Moderate risk

Can you:
- insure against these things happening?
- avoid these events by anticipating for them?

High Risk

You must be able to:
- Avoid
- Mitigate
- Insure against, or
- Reduce

these effects, otherwise your investment may be a disaster

Small Effect

Small Risk

Do not spend too much time worrying about things here. Focus your efforts elsewhere.

Moderate Risk

Too many small events can build up to a big effect. Are these things related or likely to happen together? How might you mitigate some or all of those effects?

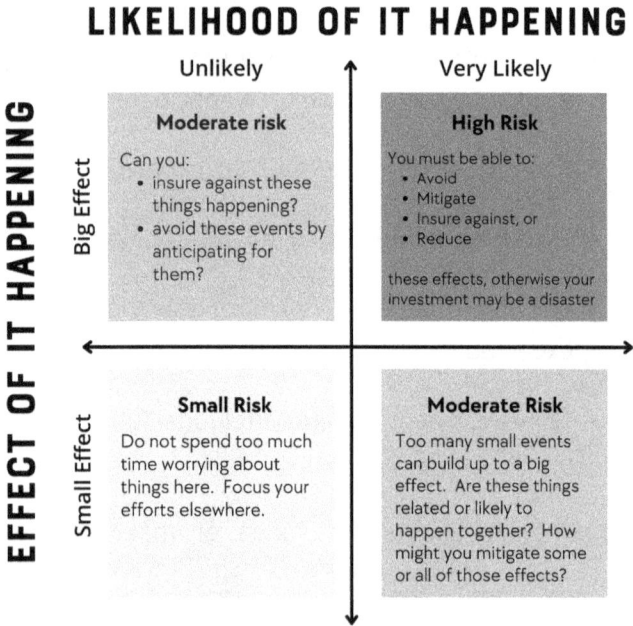

Finally – is there anyone who can give you another perspective? The greatest risks are the ones we are not even aware of. How can you get a reliable third party to check your blind spots? When we think of a decisive person, we often get the impression that they make snap decisions. But the best decisions are not made in a hurry. They take a bit of time and consideration of all the complexity.

N OW YOU HAVE COMPLETED this chapter, you will have a better understanding of whether your decisions align with your values, how active your inner critic may be in making you doubt your own knowledge and how to clarify some of the risks that you face in your financial choices. That's a lot!

The power of the exercises in the chapter does not come from using one over the other, but rather using them all together to gain a richer understanding of the decisions you are considering.

By taking your time to think about the information you have available, you will be able to tune into whether a financial risk is worthwhile for you right now, or not.

A great financial decision is not one which is simple to make – but one in which you have considered all your angles, taken action to reduce your risk, and made a thoughtful decision which aligns with your values.

Have a look back at the Money Pizza in Chapter 1 and your answer to I Am Happy To Make Financial Decisions. Having read this chapter, would you change your initial response? You are probably more aware of the complexity of financial decision making, and have a little more understanding about why your brain might struggle with these decisions.

When you find yourself overwhelmed by the possibilities, come back to this chapter to help clarify your thinking. You are the expert in your life and very often, you are the best person to make these decisions. Trust yourself and your knowledge.

CHAPTER SEVEN

Financial Flexibility

"The path to your success is not as fixed and inflexible as you think."

Misty Copeland

B EING AT EASE WITH money is often due to the critical mindset of being financially flexible. Living well within our means, so there is some wriggle room even with limited cashflow. On the other hand, we feel stuck financially when we find we are dependent on a certain income to maintain our lifestyles. If this is the case for you, it can seem like there is no imaginable way to restart a career, or rethink where and how you live – because you seem stuck financially.

Reading this chapter will help you recognise where you might be at risk of becoming financially inflexible. You will be able to identify decisions today that may turn into future burdens and, importantly, learn how to avoid, mitigate or recover from these decisions.

You might feel you are financially inflexible if you find yourself thinking you have to suck it up at work because you are being paid above market rates. Or, you could find yourself putting off life until retirement, when the prospect of a pension is due to pay off. Perhaps you find yourself resisting doing any research about other options for where to live, work and how you spend your money because you believe you are too old to change. Or, you continue on the path you started on decades ago, because that is all you can imagine yourself doing. And yet, you are filled with a quiet regret. Financial inflexibility can also present as something more indirect. You may find yourself spending all your money and time on other people, or letting other people influence where and how your money is invested. If you see yourself in any of these situations, understand there is a way to become more flexible.

What is financial flexibility?

Financial flexibility means being able to change your lifestyle and work, when you want, without being held back by your finances. In business, financial flexibility is reduced when a company takes on too much debt or has too many fixed costs. The same holds true for your personal finances. Financial flexibility also decreases when you are over-reliant on one income – or your fixed costs increase to the point where you are covering your obligations with little room for discretionary spending, saving and investing.

In complete contrast, being financially flexible allows you to respond quickly when life throws you a curveball. For example, you may unexpectedly start a family (trust me, it happens); find you can no longer continue your chosen career; have a health scare; or fall in love with someone who lives on the other side of the world.All of these scenarios require a wholesale rethinking of your entire life, including your finances.

Additionally, being financially flexible reduces the volatility in your financial life. If housing payments are eating up too much of your income – any small economic shock can become a big problem.

What keeps you stuck financially?

There are many things that could be keeping you stuck – or maybe just one big thing. Consider the following list:

- Your fixed costs (usually housing) are so high that you don't feel you can leave your job.

- You take on too much debt (big mortgages, I'm looking at you).

- You feel you must follow a particular career

because you have spent a shit load of time and money training for it (university costs are a big contributor here).

- You don't have any emergency funds to help you in a tight situation (a credit card is not an emergency fund).

- You never use debt because you are afraid of it and, therefore, never purchase those significant income producing assets.

- You are over reliant on your employer (for example, for a final salary pension, being so safe in your job you don't keep your skills up-to-date or consider changing to a role you enjoy).

- You never invest because you believe it's gambling.

- You only work with what you already know and believe, never challenging your limiting beliefs or mental blocks.

These are all sticky situations and if you have any of them, I advise you to work on one thing at a time. You may notice it is about changing your mindset; no surprises there. But there are significant practicalities to consider too.

Avoid high fixed costs

High fixed costs for most people revolve around housing (but childcare can be a whopper if you have children too). There is an imbalance of supply and demand for rental housing stock in large cities from London to Sydney to San Francisco. This means that landlords can charge their tenants ridiculous rents. When your housing costs chew up more than 50 per cent of your take home pay, managing outgoings becomes unsustainable.

However, I often see people about to purchase a home who consider overstretching themselves in the same way. They are so desperate to shorten their commuting time that they are willing to sacrifice a significant portion of their income and take on astronomical piles of debt. I am a city lover and find myself drawn to the most expensive cities in the world.I've lived in Hong Kong and London and sought career changes in New York and Singapore. Short of living in Tel Aviv, Paris or Zurich, I couldn't find any more expensive places to want to live. So, I understand the drive – but also recognise it has had a significant impact on my finances and how much I spend on housing.

You may find you have made a significant property decision, which you find tricky to unwind.Not only because of the difficulty of selling, but because of the emotional attachment you have to the property.

Davina's holiday home anchor story

Davina (43) is a working mum, living with Theo (6 years old). She feels stuck in her corporate job and is considering what she needs to do to become more flexible.

"When we first had Theo, my husband and I stopped travelling because we found it too hard. Theo was very active, so dealing with planes, airports, and crowds was a nightmare. We had the opportunity to purchase a holiday flat by the sea –a lifesaver for us at the time. We enjoyed trips away and we didn't feel stuck in our innercity home. When international travel was impossible in 2020 and 2021, we enjoyed our little staycations. It was beneficial to us.

"However, now that Theo is older and life is getting back to normal – the holiday home is becoming more of a burden. We have had some great times there, but equally we want to travel more. We are spending money on the upkeep of the flat, not to mention the mortgage that we still have against it. It's not huge but it is another thing to consider.

"I was always brought up to believe that rent money is dead money. But I am rethinking that right now. What if we sold the holiday home and rented somewhere when we want a holiday? That sounds a bit radical – but it would probably work. I feel guilty about the idea of selling; we

thought we would use that place forever. It's such a luxury to have a holiday home. But now we are all getting bored of it and it seems to limit our choices.

"When I wrote down on paper how much time and money we put into maintaining the holiday flat it was significant. We could afford to rent luxury places instead, if we booked in advance.And I wouldn't have to do the cleaning up afterwards either! Or, we could go overseas. I hadn't considered overseas travel as a possibility before."

Davina worked out her holiday home was acting as more of an anchor than an asset. It reduced the family's options when they wanted to start doing things differently.

Iron rice bowls and golden handcuffs

In the Chinese tradition, an iron rice bowl refers to an occupation with guaranteed job security, reasonable pay, and perks. Sometimes it comes along with a certain level of socio-economic status as well. You may have grown up in a household which valued securing a job for life. Or, you may have a guaranteed (or final salary pension) in your current role. Sometimes companies are more explicit and offer golden handcuff packages, designed to be so attractive you are almost guaranteed to stay in an undesirable role because your pay packet is too large to leave behind.

Do you wish you had a job like that? Or does the idea of being shackled to a job make you feel uncomfortable?

In my experience – with clients and colleagues – the iron rice bowl is not as much of a blessing as expected. Because people feel they are on a good ticket, there is a strong inertia keeping them in place. You may find you are stuck in a job because the pay is so good, and you can't imagine any other opportunities out there that could be as lucrative. I have seen many colleagues who yearn for a career change but are too scared to leave a final salary pension or the significant pay package. They cannot imagine life without that so-called 'financial security' but, in reality, the security becomes more of a prison.Year after year, I see these energetic, imaginative people shrink into their jobs – too scared to consider what life might be like in a different industry or environment. Too afraid to put their financial rewards at risk, they find it impossible to consider another way of living and working.

Your job – and your lucrative pay package – may be working against your financial flexibility. Because it's too financially scary to consider changing jobs, people become inflexible in their thinking. The big risk in relying on your iron rice bowl is that – too often – it breaks.

Nat's learning flexibility story

Nat (52) is an industrial engineer by training who works in process improvement at a large multinational company.

She is based in the Midlands, UK and has enjoyed a
long career with her company. Having worked through
the ranks and the departments of her company, she
appreciates the development and support her employer
has given her.

> *"This has been the only company I have known and I
> appreciate how supportive they have been through my
> life. I don't like to think about leaving and, in any case,
> I would be walking away from a final salary pension. I
> haven't enjoyed being part of the company for the last
> three years, and I am just trying to make it until I can
> take early retirement. There is talk about restructuring in
> the future and I don't know if I want to be part of the
> restructured organisation. But I would be daft to walk
> away from the final salary pension, right?"*

As Nat continued her conversation the association
between the company and family became very clear to
her. The company was a source of support and conflict
and she felt deeply resentful of the idea that she couldn't
(in her words) walk away from a final salary pension.
I asked her to be specific about what the final salary
pension meant. If she walked away, would she forfeit all of
it? Did she know what would happen to the pension if she
were made redundant? Nat realised that she had never
questioned the received wisdom that it would be crazy to
move from a job with a final salary pension. She resolved

to find out more from her company to prepare herself for a possible redundancy.

After a few weeks, we met again and Nat updated me.

> *"I now have a better idea of my pension arrangements. I didn't realise I could keep most of what had been invested on my behalf, even when I left the company. So, I will always have some pension from my company and the small state pension I am entitled to. I had been using the idea of the pension to keep me tied to the company. I have many more choices now to look at, how I might start another way of saving money for my retirement. I could move to another company or start my own independent practice. All I need to do is keep earning money for the next 12-13 years – which I am pretty sure I can – and I will have a comfortable retirement.It's changed completely how I look at the next part of my career."*

Simply questioning the assumptions she had made about her retirement pot spurred Nat to do her research and clarify her options. When the next round of redundancies is offered, she will no longer be fearful about her future.

Giving away your money power

A new field of fascinating research – Cultural Finance – is showing that the cultures within which we grow up, live, and work significantly affect our financial literacy and willingness to make financial decisions. Particularly interesting is the observation that cultures valuing authority and hierarchy encourage people to surrender financial decisions to family members with more power and authority. This means that in more traditional structures, women give way to decisions made by men, and younger people defer to older people.

If you grew up in such an environment, you may have a strong desire for someone else to make allthe financial decisions for you. Instead of berating yourself for being financially irresponsible, look at this as a product of your culture. Give yourself the grace to understand that, like many other forms of social conditioning, this urge runs deep and is pervasive. But it can be changed and you can take back your money power.

Sometimes, this may be as simple as resisting the temptation to give away your money, to pay for other people, and to serve others before you serve yourself. Other times, it involves building your own confidence in decision making and developing your assertiveness.

What is sure is this: the more you give away your decision-making power, the less financially flexible you will become. Pay attention to the urge to push a decision to someone else. It is only an urge, and will eventually pass.

Exercise – Warning Signs Of Financial Inflexibility

Use the following exercise to work out if you are at risk of becoming financially stuck. How many of the following statements do you agree with?

- You are uneasy about your current and future financial situation.

- You fight about money matters with your spouse or most significant family member.

- You never seem to pay down your credit card debt in full.

- You use credit as your emergency fund instead of having cash.

- Losing an income means you cannot pay your living costs.

- The idea of a financial emergency makes you panic or block out any thoughts about it (denial).

- You feel uneasy when special occasions like Christmas, weddings, or other social celebrations come around.

- You do not like spending money on other people.

- You do not like spending money on yourself.

- You can't imagine that saving money could become a habit.

- You are concerned about what others think about you, the house you live in, the clothes you wear, and how well brought up your children are.

- You have to plan carefully how and when you pay the bills because your cash flow is tight.

- You are not making any savings for future expenditures, like your own or your children's education expenses.

- Debt payments (including mortgage payments) take more than 40 per cent of your household income.

- Property maintenance takes a significant (more than 10 per cent) proportion of your income and spare time each month.

- Large purchases create a damaging hole in your finances.

- You cannot imagine paying off any debt faster than the minimum payments required.

- You do not have any method to keep track of your outgoings.

- You hope life will continue as it is without planning for the unexpected.

- Any assets you buy lose value (for example, cars, sound systems, technology, clothes) and you do not have many assets that grow in value over time.

- You are constantly searching for a get-rich-quick scheme or buying lottery tickets in the hope a magical event will get you out of your financial worries.

- You see your spouse's decisions or children's needs as the main reason you cannot earn or save money.

Do your answers make you comfortable or uneasy? What does that tell you? Do you see a pattern in any of your responses?

Having gone through this list, do you feel like you are generally financially flexible, or have a few red flags been raised? You may never have thought of yourself as financially inflexible, but you may now realise there are patterns in your thinking or behaviour, which are keeping you stuck.

Is there an area you have discovered that you could focus on improving? If so, what would be the next small step you could make?

Exercise – Where Are You Feeling Stuck?

Think about the following slices of the Money Pizza: Income; Outgoings; Cash Buffer; Investments; and Use of Debt. Are there any areas where you feel 'Things are going well right now' on the surface but deep down you are not sure?

For example:

> My income is good, but I don't know what I'd do if I lost my job.

> We are on top of our outgoings, and putting some money into savings, but I don't know if we can manage the forecast cost of living increases.

> My Cash Buffer is good, but it could be spent pretty quickly.

> I have investments, but they are mostly funded by debt.

> The debt is manageable as long as interest
> rates don't go up too much.

If any of these phrases sound like something you may say, sit down and consider your plan A if things go wrong. And then consider a Plan B if things go very wrong, and Plan C and so on.

Can you make any adjustments to your plans right now to increase your flexibility and decrease the likelihood of getting stuck?

Can you adjust your spending down?

Can you increase your income through negotiation?

Can you sell investments that are a burden on your time and cash flow?

The point of completing this exercise is to start considering options and opportunities. Being financially flexible helps you become more optimistic, and that optimism will make you more receptive to new ideas and ways of behaving.

Flexibility is the key

My dad's birthday recently had a zero at the end of it. For as long as I have known him, he has been active and played squash, but has always complained about how stiff and sore he is. He embarrassed me by trying to do his stretches as we waited in line at the supermarket, with accompanying groans of dismay from both me (and him). This haphazard stretching routine of a couple of minutes, when he remembered, was not helping him make any progress. It still had the power to embarrass his adult daughter, but he was struggling to keep up with his active grandchildren.

"I'm getting old," he muttered and left it at that. We both assumed he would never touch his toes again.

When I last visited him (after three years of no international travel) he pulled me aside and said, "Look at this!" and bent over and touched his toes. I was suitably impressed. Like him, I had thought it was inevitable that he would never get close to touching his toes again. His secret? Once a week, for one hour, he did a yoga class. With guidance, practice, and the firm cajoling of his wife, dad had improved his flexibility in a reasonably short time. It was a great reminder for me that while making a change or improvement might seem impossible and the goal might feel out of reach, you are never too old, and never too stuck to change. And it really helps to have your friends and family onside too.

You might feel stuck now with your finances, but with consistency, effort and the support of your loved ones, you can become flexible again.

LOOK BACK TO THE Money Pizza once more and see how you rated yourself on the statement I Am Financially Flexible. Do you see the possibility of making further improvements?

If there is one area that you would like to improve, what is it? What obstacles might appear in the future? Who could help you keep your goals on track?

A little change here can make a big difference and consistency is key. Practice regularly seeking out different points of view and behaviours. Change your spending habits so your outgoings are reduced. Negotiate your fixed costs (rent, mortgage and utilities) and seriously consider whether a housing move could be beneficial for your cashflow.

Being flexible and financially successful is within your grasp.

CHAPTER EIGHT

Ask For What You Want

"People say that money is not the key to happiness. But I always figured if you have enough money, you can have a key made."

Joan Rivers

THIS CHAPTER IS A wake-up call to you when it comes to claiming your worth. It gives you pointers about where to look for the value you might not be claiming – yet. This chapter will help you understand what might be holding you back from asking for more and provide one or two strategies which you can pursue to boost your income. We will run through the basics of asking for more (negotiation) in any scenario, not just at work. The chapter finishes with a selection of ideas for you to consider about how you can leverage what you already know to sustainably supplement your income. It is time to stop thinking that asking for pay which supports your living standards, negotiating a pay rise, or optimising your benefits is greedy, complaining or ungrateful. When we take care of ourselves financially we have more capacity to be productive at work, as well as being generous and supportive to other people.

Why is it easier to negotiate for others?

Neuroscience offers a fascinating way to understand why we might find it almost impossible to ask for more for ourselves. Have you found you are uncomfortable when you consider asking for something for yourself, but strangely enough, you can do it on behalf of a friend, a colleague or a child? Did you ever have those awkward teenage conversations when you liked someone, but had to get one of your friends to ask them out on your behalf? That's the feeling I'm talking about.

When we negotiate on behalf of other people, we do not feel that we are in danger or that our ego could be bruised. We can maintain calm; set out our arguments and requirements; and basically, be a negotiation genius. Rebuttals are rarely taken personally, we can sit and discuss ideas and options, and it is much easier to keep emotion in check.

But when we are involved in the negotiation ourselves our body has automatic reactions that can make us feel extremely uncomfortable. We enter into the negotiation in a mental and physical state of high alert looking for threats, and our body picks up signals that our conscious mind barely recognises. At our human core, we all want to feel safe (physically and psychologically); be accepted; feel like we belong to a group; have a sense of control; feel a connection with others (including the other negotiator); and minimise potential pain. All of these aspects support a deep need for safety and, when we feel safe, our brain is able to access its higher skills of problem solving and decision making.

Yet, the slightest trigger can flick the danger switch in our brain – unleashing the fight-flight-freeze or the tend-and-befriend reactions in our body. Tend-and-befriend was identified as a stress reaction by researchers from the University of California and written up in 2000 in the Journal of the American Psychological Association. The researchers argued that behaviourally, females' stress responses have a pattern of tending (actions designed to protect the self, promote safety and reduce distress) and befriending (the creation and maintenance of social networks) that aid in the process of 'tending'. Fascinating, right?

Fight-flight-freeze shuts down your ability to speak clearly, increases your feelings of anxiety and undermines any performance. Tend-and-befriend, on the other hand, may lead you to acquiesce and give up those points of negotiation which you had planned – in an effort to maintain your connection with the other negotiator. It may encourage you to give more ground to the other party in an effort to 'befriend' and keep them happy (at your expense).

If we feel we are being greedy or ungrateful when we ask for a higher rate of pay – it can be processed as a threat to our personal identity – and can activate our bodies' stress response. This makes it difficult to start negotiating for ourselves. It is time to turn the story around and recognise that asking for more for ourselves is an act of advocacy – not only for us, but for the people who come after us. It is activism for those who struggle to speak up or who have no voice at all. Remember because you are asking for more holiday, more flexibility, more pay, more leave – you are not trying to take it away from someone else. Negotiation is not a zero-sum game. You can gain, without creating a loss for someone else.

Jenny's negotiation story

Jenny (35) worked in a largely male-oriented workplace. When she fell pregnant with her first child, she was so relieved to be able to keep her job that she did not negotiate her maternity leave.

> *"I was way too scared to negotiate anything. When I told the HR manager that I was expecting a baby, she said that she had to dust off the policy because I was the first person who would be using it! I took what was given to me, and did not complain. I was mute."*

"The leave was inadequate, but I came back to work and tried not to mention anything about my child in case it was seen as a weakness. A couple of years later, another lady who had joined the company came to ask for my advice and I shared my experience with her. She was also scared about her job prospects if she was to fall pregnant. I realised that by not negotiating earlier, I had put this woman in the same place that I had been in, and I felt terrible about not having spoken up.

"I decided that, while I had missed the opportunity to negotiate for myself, I would go back to HR and tell them why the parental leave policy should be changed. And I decided to go all in and ask for everything I could think of.

"I asked for a gold-plated maternity leave policy with 12 months' full pay. And I also argued that men should be entitled to the same rights as women. Of course, that option went down like a lead balloon, but it set the expectations really high. I found information about what other companies were offering their employees, and research from the World Health Organisation about how longer maternity leave benefits the physical and mental health of both mother and baby. I made the case as compelling as I could.

"I was still terrified. I felt that the company would think I was planning another baby, and that I was only trying to

set myself up. In the end, the company met me halfway on maternity leave (which was a huge improvement) and doubled their paternity leave allowance to two weeks.

"I never wanted to be an activist, but now I find myself arguing for better flexibility for all parents. Keeping in mind the newcomers and younger staff members who will join the company in the future made the negotiation easier. Along with excellent preparation and practice, of course! I keep telling everyone – male or female – that they owe it to the next generation to negotiate for themselves now."

Get what's coming to you – in the nicest possible way

The easiest way to optimise your income is to claim what you are already entitled to ... but which you might not know about. These aspects can include the following:

1. Pension contribution matching;

2. Checking your benefits;

3. Taking advantage of perks;

4. Using your leave allowance, including unpaid leave if that works for you.

Private pension (superannuation) contribution matching

Many companies now use enhanced employer pension contributions to attract and retain people[1]. In the UK, employers are required to contribute a minimum of 3 per cent to your personal pension on top of the minimum contributions you make. However, if your company has a contribution matching scheme, which relies on you to increase your pension contributions, then increase your contributions. Do it now!

Not only will you be making pre-tax contributions (which will reduce the amount of tax you pay), the matching from your company amounts to free money going into your long-term investments. There are limits on the amounts you can contribute pre-tax, and these change each year. If you know you are in the highest tax bracket, it is worth checking these limits before you make any changes.

The contribution matching is extra money which helps add to the compounding effect of any interest you earn on your pension amount. It is kept out of reach so you won't

---

1. In Australia and New Zealand, private pension savings schemes are generally called superannuation programs ('super' for short) – and it should be noted that most of the information here refers to UK pension requirements. If you live in a different country, use these suggestions as starting points for discussions, and get a friendly human resources person to help you out with legal requirements.

be tempted to spend it and you will be quietly building your long-term investments. I vote for that.

Check your benefits

Does your company offer health insurance? Do you use it? I know people who feel like it is a betrayal of their local health system if they decide to use private health providers. Please, never let this be you.

It is not shameful or a betrayal of the amazing NHS (UK) or Medicare (Australia) systems if you decide to use your health insurance to gain access to private services. When you take yourself out of the queue for public services, you make a place in the free system available for someone who may not have access to the private benefits you have.

Take the plunge and ask if your company can extend the private health insurance to your family. This can be invaluable, especially when you have a young family. Use these benefits as much as you can to support your own health; whether that means regular check-ups or receiving specialised therapy to deal with a niggling issue. Maintaining your mental strength and physical health is so valuable – because you are the golden goose. And you may prevent costly treatment in years to come.

Are you entitled to a car? If you have space available to park it (not always easy, I know) you may be able to cut down on household running costs by taking advantage of a company car. In addition, if you are using the car a lot for work, you may be able to claim back mileage from your company or against your tax costs.

Finally, does your company provide life insurance for you, and can it extend to your family? Many companies will have a policy that provides a payout if you become ill and cannot work, or if you die while you are still in employment. (Note: this is different to a fatality due to work.) This is a valuable form of insurance if you have a family and/or outstanding debts like a mortgage on a home, and it is worthwhile to check if you are already covered.

Are you taking advantage of perks?

These can include: flexible hours; working-from-home; access to training and development; being issued company shares; financial wellness programs (yeah!); and paid-for holidays. If these items are offered in your workplace – lucky you! Make sure you use them, otherwise you are literally leaving money on the table.

If you don't take paid leave – you're stupid. Harsh? Perhaps. But I believe it's true. I know companies where it's a badge of honour if you don't take any holiday throughout the year. The idea is that you are super tough and holidays are for the weak of heart and body. I suggest if you think this, you have control-freak tendencies. You are foolish to be working for free for two to four weeks each year. This goes for working while you are on paid annual leave too.

You. Are. Working. For. Free.

If you do not take your entire leave allowance each and every year you are likely to be on a road to burnout. Anyway, would it be so bad if the office blew up without you? Perhaps they need to experience why they should do their best to keep you, by having two weeks of regular chaos while you are away. This will give you more ammunition to negotiate a better salary later because the cost of your leaving for good – or being truly burnt-out – would be too high for the company to manage.

Perhaps what you need is more time off work. Are there any options for unpaid leave you can take advantage of? Perhaps it's time for a sabbatical? It doesn't need to be hugely long to have a refreshing effect on your performance at work. If you are entitled to this kind of leave, it can be a great advantage to take it.

How to prepare for a negotiation

It always pays (quite literally) to prepare for a negotiation. Even if the other side is friendly, you are much better off having as much information as possible. It is your responsibility to inform yourself, and a lot of that information comes from your own head. Let's write it down on paper to be very clear about this aspect.

Would you like to earn AU$5,000 (GBP 2,500) in an hour? This is how Scott Pape, the Barefoot Investor, looks at negotiating your pay. He argues that if you earn AU$50,000 (he is Australian after all, so we will use AU$ to be culturally appropriate) and manage to negotiate a 10 per cent pay rise (or comparable uplift in benefits), you will have earned a tidy sum in that one hour of negotiation.

How much discomfort are you willing to put yourself under for that one hour? How much would it be worth to you? Would you pick up a non-venomous snake for GBP 2,500? How about a spider? Negotiating a pay rise can make you just as uncomfortable or scared – and if the result is 'no' it might hurt your ego, but you won't die from it. So, try to quantify how much value you could gain from an hour of negotiation and make a decision. You decide whether or not it will be worth it.

Expressed like that, you may find you can manage a certain amount of discomfort. But you do not have to brazen it out. Read on for the best negotiation tools to use.

What is your Best Alternative To A Negotiated Agreement (BATNA)?

This is what will happen or what you will have, even if you do not succeed with the negotiation. If this is the status quo, make sure you write down important information, such as the following.

- How much are you paid in salary and bonuses?
  Be as precise as possible. Note down before and
  after-tax amounts.

- How many hours a week/month/year do you
  work?

- Can you work out what your equivalent hourly rate
  is?

- Are you entitled to overtime payments? If so, what
  are the terms?

- Do you have any pension matching arrangements
  or share options?

- How many days of paid holiday do you have in a
  year?

- Can you work out what your holidays are worth
  per day?

Write down as much detail as you can about your status
quo. And if you are unemployed, consider all the different
activities you could do with that time. You could: recover
and relax; retrain and find another career; connect with
family and friends who you have not had time for. Time is
precious too – it is important to remind yourself of that.

Remember it is unlikely you will be fired for simply trying
to negotiate a pay rise. Apart from being morally dubious,
companies risk legal action if such activities are seen to be

discriminatory. Many jurisdictions have laws against such moves.

What is your Reserve Value?

What is the lowest rate of pay, number of holidays and all the extra stuff that you require in order to adequately compensate you for taking the risk of starting a new position? If you are already in a job – what would make you leave? Really? I once tried to negotiate for flexible working (this was pre-pandemic), and was rebuffed by the company. I did not leave immediately – but it was a significant factor in my longer-term decision to leave that company, which I eventually did two years later. Flexible working was an important part of my Reserve Value – and I eventually walked away because I didn't get it.

What is your Target Value?

This is your wish list. Achieving everything you want should be your goal, your 'absolutely everything' value. It can be very useful to put down all you find valuable in a negotiation – especially so you can filter any offers made to you as not being worthwhile.

For example, you might want a free canteen at lunchtime and low-cost personal loans (some banks offer these). If the company turns around instead and offers you a car and free yoga classes – and these are not attractive to you (because, for example, you don't drive in the city and hate wearing lycra in public) – you can easily explain that these offers are not appealing for you.

The Target Value is different from what you think you are likely to receive. It should be better than your BATNA, ambitious and at the same time, something the other side could potentially agree to.

Fei's negotiation story

After a year of intense work for a Hong Kong hedge fund, Fei (35) found herself unexpectedly out of a job.

"I was working at this fund, and I absolutely loved it. The atmosphere was fizzing, and we were constantly busy. The problem was, we weren't closing any deals. I didn't think much of it at the time – which I realise was naive – because I thought I would have another year to prove my worth. Anyway, one day during lunch I realised the boss was firing me. And just like that I was out of a job. It was amicable, and I was able to choose the manner in which I left. But it was clear that I was out for good.

"I found myself without much of a plan, but fortunately with enough money to take some time off. I was not in a hurry to return to work because I had been shocked to find my longed-for hedge fund career seemed like a non-starter. After a month, I was contacted by an old

colleague. Long story short: they wanted to offer me a job in my old industry. I wasn't excited by it, but I didn't have any other options on the horizon. I decided since I had time on my hands, I would prepare for the negotiation process as well as possible. I worked out my Best Alternative to a Negotiated Agreement (BATNA) was the status quo. I had enough money to survive a year of living simply – and frankly, I could have done with the time off. It didn't seem such a bad prospect at all. Or, I could always go out and find another job.

"My Reserve Value was the minimum income I was willing to accept, to compensate for the fact I was missing out on a year's sabbatical, which I felt I really needed. I had a number in mind, and it was actually a higher salary than I had been on. My Target Value was significantly higher than my previous salary. I decided since the new company didn't offer bonuses, I could aim for multiples of my previous salary.

"Then, I wrote down all the extras which I would have liked: the maximum days' annual leave (which I knew my friend had); health insurance; pension matching contribution; business class travel for all my work trips; and three months of unpaid leave so I could have a mini-sabbatical within the first year of joining. I know – they sound ridiculous – but I figured I had nothing to lose. If this negotiation didn't work, I still had a year off ahead of me.

"My opening salary pitch was going to be HK$75,000 per month – an astronomical number for me. I practised saying the number in the mirror so I wouldn't stumble on the words. But with the preparation I had made, and the knowledge that my BATNA (being unemployed for another year) was actually really attractive – I felt comfortable. Yes, you could say I felt safe going into the negotiation.

"I opened the negotiation by explaining how it was wonderful to talk to them, but I was not actively looking for a position at the moment. As the discussions developed, I mentioned all of the non-salary related perks in which I was interested. Pensions, holidays, business class travel etc. The company must have been impressed by my calmness and my preparation – and I knew that sitting around negotiating tables was an important part of the new job.

"When we actually talked about salary numbers I was a little disappointed after the meeting. So, I was surprised when they called back and offered me almost twice what I was going to open with! The only aspects they refused were the business class travel and pension contributions, which were both company-wide policies. I figured with the extra money, I could pay for those myself.

"That was an important lesson about turning a position of weakness (unemployment) into a strength (a sabbatical)

*in my own mind. I was really comfortable about
walking away from the table without a deal – and it
helped me stay calm. The preparation really helped.
They knew I had done my research – so made me an
offer I couldn't refuse. And I didn't!"*

Make a bit on the side

I am not a great fan of the side hustle because I
don't like the idea that we need to work all hours of
the day. However, I believe we each have far more
valuable knowledge captured in our brains which can
help other people. And when I say valuable, I mean
valuable. You will be amazed that what you might
think is dead simple (cake decorating, knowing how
to properly prepare a wall for painting, maintaining a
bicycle, etc.) is a complete mystery to other people.
I will also go against the grain and say you can start
doing these activities in person with other people.
Becoming an internet video star is not everyone's cup
of tea but helping out your local community for a
tenner may well be something which lights you up.

Would you be willing to put a sign up at the local pub
and advertise that you will do quick bike maintenance
while people are having a pint? This seems far more
low-key and a safer risk than buying the kit to make
professional-looking videos. I realise this is my own bias

coming to the fore. I hate recording videos and rely on a group of other people to help me with them.

As a recovering sew-a-holic, I also understand the financial pitfalls of turning your hobby into a source of income. Many hobbies like sewing, craft, candle making etc. can turn into money black holes as you buy more and more equipment and supplies. Consider carefully if you want to be stocking and selling things before you jump in.

But what do you know that could be useful? What knowledge can you leverage in a personal way? Consider the following options: freelancing; coaching; running workshops; giving talks locally.

Is there a service you can provide for a few hours a week that could provide a sustainable long-term addition to your income? It doesn't have to be something which will replace your career altogether, only a complement to it for now.

How are you feeling about your income now? A little more optimistic, perhaps? What is the next thing you can do to maximise the value you can create for yourself? Choose one idea you have from reading this chapter, and set out your plan for pursuing it. I am a big fan of going for the easiest thing first – so what could it be for you?

L OOK BACK ON YOUR Money Pizza. Most people will recognise ways in which they can increase their income so they can be more satisfied with what they are earning. Would you re-rate how you feel about your income – or is there something more you need to do? Have you thought of ways you could increase your income? I conclude this chapter with Fei's final feedback to help you on your money journey.

"I realised that I felt so uncomfortable about negotiating for a pay rise and perhaps I have more work to do on myself so I don't let my feelings hold me back from making requests. However, doing the exercises of gathering my information, and really thinking about what was important to me, was actually one of the most valuable things I've done in my career. It made me think about more than just the money – even though I did focus on the numbers a lot.

"I know that everyone has their own way of negotiating – so I understand there is no 'one right way' for me to conduct these conversations. But now I have been successful in this negotiation, it gives me hope for the future and what else I can achieve."

Chapter Nine

Manage Your Outgoings

"If diets and budgets actually worked, we'd all be skinny and rich."

Me

W HEN I STARTED TO live with higher costs on a lower income due to the wondrous delight of having a baby, I discovered an app called, You Need A Budget. WTF? I asked myself. Do weight loss companies run around with apps called, You Need A Diet? However, a loud voice inside me was telling me I needed an itemised budget to work out my chaotic life. Everyone who is good with their money is great at budgeting. Right?

On the other hand, the budget-diet association was a strong one for me. Diets have always been about restriction, 'bad' foods, calorie counting and – ultimately – failure. I couldn't articulate it at the time, but the same feeling of restriction and failure overcame me when I thought about budgeting!

However – and this stretches the diet-budget analogy a bit further – exactly like eating well and knowing about good nutrition, you absolutely need to know where your money is coming from and where it is going. Although this knowledge is essential, I don't believe strict and detailed budgeting is the best, or only tool, you can use.

Myths about budgeting

Every now and then, thoughtless trolls with a public platform declare people who struggle to make ends meet 'just need to learn how to budget, and be more careful about where their money is going'. That is bonafide bullshit thinking. You cannot budget your way out of poverty. If you do not have enough money to cover your basic needs, such as: housing; utilities; food; transport; clothing; education; and the additional small items that make a life – no amount of mindful consumption is going to get you out of that hole.

A key factor I have learned from my work in money behaviour is this: the best way to learn how to budget is to have no disposable income. How would you feel about that? When every dollar matters, you make every dollar work. When I talk about this with my friends, they all say they were better at budgeting – nay, ingenious – when they were poor students just out of school, but they lost that precious skill as soon as a disposable income appeared in their lives.

This idea is reinforced by the work I have completed with money and debt advice charities. A strong message I received was, 'We don't need to teach our clients how to budget. Most of them know exactly where every pound goes. They are super aware of what they are spending their money on, and why.'

Please, never tell someone on a low income they need to learn how to budget. They can probably do it in their sleep. Ask a starving person what they think about most – it's food. Ask people with a low income what they think about the most – it's money. Where the next dollar will come from and where it goes. If you want to understand what it means to be truly mindful about every dollar you spend – and how much stress that can put on your wellbeing – get a job on a minimum wage and try to survive. It is difficult and stressful.

Budgeting is a learned skill. Some people have learned to be very skilful at budgeting because – you guessed it – they learned to do so at home. Either they saw their parents being extremely careful with money – or budgeting was essential to be able to survive growing up. Budgeters learn to be thrifty because they must be, not because they have a choice.

It is an irony that the people who tend to struggle with budgeting the most are those (like me) who have had the advantage of disposable income for most of their lives. This means you can buy yourself little (and large) luxuries, such as: toys; nice shoes; branded items; electronics; and books. In fact, much of what we think are essentials are luxuries that we have grown to expect in our daily lives. Computers and smart phones are one example. Imagine if you had to give up one or both of these essential tools? For me, it doesn't bear thinking about.

Please – stop thinking you are morally lacking or a bad person if you find it hard to budget. Take a moment to recognise this is probably because you were never forced to survive on the bare minimum. Sit with this idea, for a moment and enjoy the fact you are probably quite well off. Read this chapter with curiosity about what you can learn, and strategies you can try.

Spending

Spending is emotional. Learn to deal with the emotions and you can manage your spending better. Do I sound like a broken record, yet? I hope so. Remember your behaviours are driven by your thoughts, and your thoughts are interwoven with your emotions. Many budgeting techniques are based only on cognition – those rational economic thoughts you actually notice – or some behavioural adjustments. While these techniques are useful they only really deal with the surface level issues.

Firstly, work out what your emotional baggage is. Part of understanding this is working out if you have a 'thing' about budgeting (like I have) and also why you spend the way you do. Decide what you want to change (if anything) and why it is important to you to change that aspect of your spending.

Secondly, choose strategies and methods that suit you. It is important to understand there is no one-size-fits-all method which works for everyone. Work out what fits your lifestyle and start incorporating that into your financial habits. You may be tempted to try to control everything – but I do not recommend it. Big personal development projects can become overwhelming and your enthusiasm may flame out.

Rather than budgeting for everything all at once – tackle one aspect of your life at a time. If you think your grocery spending needs some control, set a limit for today's food spend alone. Or the week, if that works for you. Start by looking at what you spend for a week, and see where you can make prudent changes. Could it be better to use a delivery service, where you won't be tempted by in-store promotions? Would it help you to write a list when you do the shopping and stick to it? Perhaps one big weekly shop be would better for your cashflow? Or you may find you waste less food if you shop every three days or so. There are pros and cons to everything. Be curious about what works best for you.

Shift your mindset

Think about controlling your spending as a mindset shift. It's not about lack of money; it's about being thoughtful. You prepare for your spend, you stick to your plan and you reap the rewards.

By the way, professionals are shit at budgeting too. Organisations are, by their own admission, crap at developing and sticking to reasonable budgets. The business world changes all the time and yet the way businesses budget doesn't seem to change. Despite an extraordinary amount of research about organisational budgeting techniques, no single effective budgeting method has been found for companies. Business academics, including Professor Péter Hováth, think traditional budgeting is counterproductive, partly because budgets quickly become outdated and do not align with company strategy. They recommend – surprise, surprise – that budgets are adapted to organisational changes and the process is refined for each different organisational unit. Anyone who has worked in a business will know this is easier said than done.

So, why the heck do we think a single budget will work for us? Our lives are as dynamic and changeable as any organisation. It follows that we need different approaches to traditional budgeting. Sticking with something – like controlling your spending and changing your behaviour

– is difficult. You need to think about it completely differently. Below are two financial mindset shifts that work for most of my clients.

Mindset shift #1

Previous mindset: People are born good at controlling their spending or not and can be divided up into 'spenders' and 'savers'.

New mindset: We can all learn how to control our spending, by making small changes, sticking at it, and being curious about our behaviour.

Mindset shift #2

Previous mindset: Budgeting is about restriction, tightening our belts and doing without the things we enjoy.

New mindset: Reframe budgeting so it doesn't have the same connotation of restriction. Never use the word 'budget' if that evokes images of Ebenezer Scrooge from A Christmas Carol. Rename the process to something else like: My Money Plan; Every Pound Has A Job; Spending Priorities; Cash Control; Spending Plan; Effective Cash Flow; Money Monitoring; Mindful Money; Money Map – or a name that works for you.

I T IS HARD TO change down a gear in spending, for example, when your income goes down. The best protection is to guard against lifestyle inflation where your spending increases in line with your income going up. This is - of course - easier said than done. But some items that can really cause a step up in lifestyle creep include: moving house; buying a place to live; travel; hobbies; cars; owning a pet; or starting a family.

What is your spending kryptonite?

Every money superhero has their kryptonite and so do you. Your weak spot could be the people, person, situation, hobby or pet on which you just can't help spending money. Read on for examples from clients, and see if any of their stories ring a bell for you.

Jamie:

"During the lockdowns in the UK, a friend of mine gave me her old sewing machine because I was bored and I wanted something to improve as my lockdown skill. I had a great time making clothes for myself and my daughter - but gee I would spend £100 for something that I could buy for a fraction of the price. Soon, internet shopping for trimmings and nice fabric became a way to pass the time, far more than actually

sewing. I had to wilfully change a spending habit that got out of control very quickly."

Sam:

"My spending kryptonite is my dog. I can't go past a doggy toy without buying it and he destroys them in minutes! I'm always buying new things for him."

Mel:

"I have a friend who I love, but I always spend more money when I'm out with her. We'll go into TK Maxx for a browse and she'll encourage me to buy everything I pick up. I feel bad if I say no, because it's like I don't value what she has to say or I'm making a judgement on her taste. I worked out that I can meet her at different locations where shopping won't be the main feature."

Dave:

"Christmas is my kryptonite, especially that last week before the holiday, where you are still at work and you see all the advertising and think, 'What if we don't have a … Terry's Chocolate Orange … Port for after the cheese … what about having the right cheeses, chutney, crackers …. how about extra treats … what do we have for the kids?' I end up spending so much in the week before Christmas and we have so many leftovers. But I also like all the excitement

about the holiday. It may sound strange, but I love shopping on Christmas Eve. I once decided to stick to a budget for Christmas. I planned ahead, everyone received presents and we had a lovely meal. But I have to admit I missed the energy and sense of panic and it didn't feel like a real Christmas to me."

Brooke:

"Weddings are my kryptonite and the social requirements can be a killer. First you want to look good, so you buy a new dress and then you realise you need shoes and a bag to go with it. Hopefully there are not strict dress codes, but often you have travel expenses, maybe staying overnight somewhere, and then a gift! It is almost impossible not to spend lots of money and when there is more than one wedding a year to go to, it gets really expensive. I don't want to not go - or not give a gift - or not look my best. Because you know the wedding itself has cost the couple so much, and you don't want to act like you don't care about your friend's big day. I have another wedding coming up and I have decided to wear exactly the same thing I wore to the last one. As one of my friends said, "Nobody is looking at you in the photos. They are looking at the bride and groom!"

Richard:

"I have a young daughter who loves clothes and toys and we love mucking around together. Every time I go shopping,

I pick up a Lego toy, or a pretty little t-shirt with sequins. The kids' stuff is never more than £10. I always anticipate the cry of 'Daddy, you are the best!' when I get home with the shopping. One day I had the groceries delivered and as I was unpacking the bags, my daughter came in and asked, 'Where is my present, Daddy?' It hadn't occurred to me until then that it had become a habit. I felt really ashamed that I hadn't thought of her and that I had established such a bad habit. She saved me and said, 'Daddy, never mind, let's play with these stickers together'. Without realising it, she had highlighted my bad habit and provided a solution. Now, I might buy her a surprise every now and then, but I make sure that we play together for ten minutes or so when I get home. That is more important to her."

How to manage your emotional spending

It is impossible to take the emotion out of how you spend your money so I am not going to ask you to do it. Instead, I want you to look at your emotions. Really look at them. Go deep and dirty with what is driving your spending. Underneath the exposure to advertising, the opportunity to spend and the habitual factors – you are trying to satisfy an emotional need by spending money. This also applies to elements of investing, employment, donations, inheritance – whenever you spend your time or your money.

In fact, any decision made about the self is emotional – and decisions around money are extremely emotional – even when you think you have those emotions under control. Emotions, which may be strong or subtle, are signals about your deeper needs that are not being met. It is so much more than how you behave.

Consider this: the best behavioural scientists in the world are usually employed by advertisers. Yes, advertisers! The experts in the field of behavioural nudges are using those nudges to their advantage and getting you to spend more with them. For example, Rory Sutherland, the compelling author of *Alchemy: The Surprising Power of Ideas That Don't Make Sense* loves behavioural science and nudges because they sell more products. He is aware of the placebo effect, and how it works with people even when they know they are taking a placebo. The book is a great introduction to behavioural science in the real world. If you want to know how advertisers attract your attention and convince you to spend, it is well worth a read.

Call to mind the work you completed in Chapter 3: Your Money Compass (if you don't remember, go back and re-do the exercises). Reconnecting with your values is a great way to build your resilience to advertising messages. One of the key ways companies entice you to spend money is by convincing you that you are getting good value. But remember – good value doesn't always mean good *values* for you.

When you find yourself tempted to purchase something which might be a 'want' more than a 'need' ask yourself if you are making a values-based decision. Of course, there will be some value to you – there always is – but does it align with your values? Does purchasing this item actually get you further towards financial independence, or does it take you a step further away? Does purchasing this item contribute towards environmental sustainability or contribute to its destruction? Does purchasing this item support your family's future, or undermine it?

If – and it's a big if – you can stop yourself from making an immediate purchase, recall and consider the values that are important to you. Not only will it help you think twice, it will also flag where you might be spending for emotional reasons.

Find your zing

Experiences that make you feel good will activate your brain's reward centre, which responds by releasing a neurotransmitter called dopamine. This naturally occurring chemical plays a key role in establishing and reinforcing habits – including bad habits – by linking the behaviour that makes you feel good with the desire to do them again.

Dopamine is that little zing you may get from buying something. Perhaps you buy a cake (zing!) and take it home to eat it (zing!). Or do you like online shopping?

Your card is charged (zing!), you get a confirmation email of your purchase, a notification of dispatch and the item eventually arrives (zing, zing, zing)!

When I worked in an office, I had a habit of indulging in a little retail therapy after particularly stressful days. This routine was assisted by the fact there were no less than ten clothing stores, five cosmetic shops, and three cake shops in the 200 meters between my office and the tube station. I could reward myself with a purchase of £2 or £200 whenever I wanted to. And – heavens – I wanted to.

This was a tough habit to break. Trying on dresses made me feel attractive. Smelling perfumes brought back good memories. Buying things made me feel especially good – for a while. But I could not justify having more clothes than would fit in my wardrobe, nor even another little cosmetic.

One workday, after tearing myself away from another possible purchase, I sat down in a huff. I had endured a pretty stressful day and wanted something to make me feel better. But not spending money made me feel deprived – I deserved a reward! The idea popped into my head that I should put the saved money aside – right now – and not wait until I had a surplus at the end of the month. I decided on a Christmas shopping saving goal. Instead of buying something in that stressful post-work moment, I opened my banking app and sent some money to a new digital saving bucket. Zing!

There it was. A little reminder that I had done something to make myself feel good. Testing out my idea during the following week, I tried on clothes (zing!), thought carefully, and every time I decided against a purchase I transferred some money into my savings bucket (zing again!). As time went by, the saving habit became easier and the spending habit waned. Replacing my spending zing with a savings zing made changing that very sticky habit much easier.

How to learn from every purchase

Remember, as we all do, you are going to make mistakes in your attempts to change your behaviour. This is good. Yes, good! That's because each time you find you have made a mistake, you can learn from it. Instead of saying to yourself, "Shit, I've done it again," think, "That's interesting, what can I learn from it?"

When you find yourself regretting a purchase after the fact, think back to the How, What and Why factors.

- How were you feeling?

- What sensations did you notice?

- Where were you?

- What did you purchase?

- Why did you want to purchase something at that point?

- How did you purchase it?

- Was there a trigger to your purchase?

- Did something or someone set you off?

Notice as many facts as you can about what happened and how you were feeling before you made the purchase. As you look through your answers, think: What does this mean for me?

In the example I gave you about my spending zing, I knew my spending was emotional and I wanted a mood boost. What does your spending mean to you? Do you have a desire for a safe, cosy and secure home? Could that be the underlying reason why you bought that lamp or plant? Do you want to feel better about your appearance – and that's why you bought those clothes? Or do you want validation for hard work which you are not receiving from your employer or colleagues? Be kind when considering what your spending means for you.

The best aspect of this process, is the 'now what' part. Now you know so much more about yourself and your spending habit – what are you going to do? You can choose to change nothing – and carry on the same way, but now you are better informed. Or, you can choose a different behaviour and try something new for you.

I like to ask myself, "What do I really want. What am I really looking for?"

"What, so what, now what" in action

Let me give you another personal example. Right now, I am a member of several study, book, coaching and networking groups. We exchange so many great ideas and good information but I can't take it all in and I become overwhelmed by other people's information and suggestions. I have to watch myself every time someone recommends a book. I love books. I love reading them and I really like buying them. But I have so many books on my bookshelf I haven't read! I know I'm not alone in this, and I still tend to buy more books than I read. What's more, most of these discussions are conducted via online video calls. So, it's no problem to open an internet browser window and purchase a book online before the discussion is even finished!

My What? My danger zone is in an online discussion with other bookworms. Alarm bells start ringing when someone recommends a book.

My So what? My deep desire is I want to know everything about everything. I want to be a world expert in whatever we are discussing. I want to look as well informed as the other people on the call and part of me hopes that buying the book will transfer the knowledge directly to my brain. In my heart, I don't believe I know enough and I am lacking in intelligence compared to the people on the online discussion. I believe buying the book is all I need to do. But I know rationally that – actually – I would be better off reading the information already available to me. Or even (whisper it) writing my own book.

My Now what? I know I'm not getting rid of my self-doubt any time soon. But what I can do is put the books in the online shopping basket and leave them for 24-48 hours. I can search my local library to see if I can borrow the book instead of buying it. If I am still determined to purchase a book, I will look for a second-hand copy. Or, I will write down the title of the book on a sticky note. If I notice it days later and it doesn't resonate with me, I throw away the sticky note. It's not a perfect system but it has cut my book buying by 80 per cent.

Automation: your secret weapon

In an age of faster and more frequent transactions, there is much to be said about slowing down your spending, and embracing the physicality of cash. However, in the post-Covid world where contactless transactions are now the norm, many shops do not take cash anymore. Additionally, the myriad digital services including deliveries and shopping that make our lives easier – especially for people who live in remote places or have mobility issues – all rely on cashless payments.

Managing our money digitally is the default for many of us. Many young people are embracing cash-only as a way to slow down and be mindful of their spending. I can only welcome this. But it is not a long-term solution, rather a short-term exercise to take stock of what money is going where.

It is now normal to manage your money online and many banks are developing tools to assist their customers with behavioural changes to make money management easier. What's my favourite trick? Automation.

This is easier if you are a salaried worker and paid regular amounts on a regular basis. For example, you can automate your private pension savings so they are taken out of your pay (pre-tax!) and go straight into your retirement pot. You don't even see the money in your bank account and you won't be tempted to spend it.

You can arrange your bills so they are paid shortly after you receive your salary. Again, the less time the money is visible in your account, the less temptation there is to spend. Pay your critical costs first. This includes: housing; food; utilities; transport to work; and communications. If you live in a city centre, the chances are your housing and essentials chew up more than 60 per cent of your income and this can make living frugally a must.

Once you have taken into account your essentials, consider how much you want to be saving or putting aside to pay down any debt. This number is different for everyone, but if you want a guide I suggest 20 per cent of your income. You could choose to have an automatic transaction which transfers 20 per cent of your take-home income to a separate account on payday. This could be an account with a different bank or share purchasing platform – or it could simply be a another digital space in your banking app. Either way: out of sight, out of mind.

If there is only a little money available to spend in your account (after you've taken care of essentials), every time you check your balance you will be more likely to stop and consider whether the immediate spend is necessary. Only having to look at one number – what you have to spend until the next time you are paid – can help simplify how you think about your disposable cash.

My final point is this, I have never had 'money left over' at the end of the month to put aside for saving. What I recommend is to start putting your money aside at the start of the month and don't touch it. If you don't want to do a wholesale spending audit, try this exercise. Put a small amount of money aside – say £10, or an amount that you would barely notice – and leave it. Next month, you can increase that saving amount to £15. Each month, see if you can increase the amount slowly – so you barely realise it's gone. You will start to create a saving habit. The amount is not the important bit but the repetition is. What could you start to put aside each month without noticing? £5? £50? What stops you from putting an automatic transfer in place, right now?

Exercise – Replace Your Spending Zing With A Savings Zing

It is time to dust off your physical moneybox or digital saving space (or create one if you don't have one). Decide on something to save for – or a debt to pay off – and name it. Put a note and/or picture of it on your moneybox. Identify one spending habit you want to break and write it down on a card or piece of paper that is in or near your wallet (or on your computer if you spend online). This will be the reminder of the new habit you want to start and the old one you want to break.

Every time you decide not to perform the habit – or spend the money – put some money in your digital saving space. If you are using physical cash, put it aside in a different part of your wallet so you can put it in your physical money box later. Keep doing this for at least a week and take note of how you feel each time. Do you get a savings zing? If not, why do you think that might be?

Exercise – Your "What, So What, Now What"

Look back at the examples I have given you in this chapter starting on page 167 and identify the triggers (What) for each purchase. Some of the triggers are emotional, others may be environmental or to do with the time of day. Use your imagination to come up with the "So What" for each person in their example. What could it mean to them? Have they identified a Now What?

Think back to a recent purchase you made and feel regret for the money you spent. Create your own case study, as if you were going to include it in this book chapter. What was the trigger for your spending? What does this mean to you? Now, what are you going to do? What might you do in the future? Write down your answers. I invite you to do this with a trusted friend. It's a great conversation starter.

T HERE IS NOTHING WRONG with making emotional spending decisions. This is how we meet our needs. But if spending has become the solution to all your emotional needs, something is out of balance. Now you know how to identify emotional spending, I invite you to make values-based decisions and notice which triggers cause you to spend more. Understanding these tools will not only help you with the small spending decisions, it will help you with the big ones too. Making a values-based decision about how and where you want to live can make a massive difference to your wallet, your family and your wellbeing.

Knowing what emotions trigger your spending can prompt you to have a deeper understanding of yourself and what is important to you. You may find you need to discuss your spending habits with family members, so they can get on board with helping you achieve your goals.

You do not have to do this alone. Spending can be a very social activity, and so can changing your behaviours. The more you can enlist support – from your friends, family and colleagues – the better you will be able to manage your spending. It can start important and honest money conversations too, and I am all about having better dialogues around money.

I invite you to flick back to the Money Pizza in Chapter 1 and have a look at the answer you gave for Outgoings. Do you have any new ideas about how you can manage your spending? Re-rate your score if you like.

This is a great chapter to refer back to if you find your spending getting a little wild. Do not worry if you need to do this – that's why it's here!

Chapter Ten

Build Your Financial Life Preserver

*"Whether the system protects or fails you, you
will be able to take care of yourself."*
                                Paulette Perhach

C ALL IT WHAT YOU will: a Fuck-Off Fund; a Running-Away
  Fund; Emergency Cash; the Freedom Fund,
whatever! If you want financial freedom and the ability to
choose the life you want, you need money you can access
at short notice. A financial life preserver is exactly that:
available money to support your life when the unexpected
happens.

But because a financial life preserver is a mouthful, let's
call it a Cash Buffer for now – but you can name it
what you like. It's your first defence against expensive

debt, unnecessary stress and being overwhelmed by life's unexpected events. Yet, too many of us fail to build a cash reserve to fall back on if we become unwell, need an urgent repair, or face unemployment.

Actual cash is no longer that easy to spend. Not long ago, I was paid in cash for a bevy of second-hand goods I had sold. I kept one crisp note as a souvenir (it was colourful and novel) and decided to deposit the rest in the bank.

Since so many shops have gone cashless it was easier to access the money in that account electronically. To my surprise, my bank had a limit on how much cash I could deposit each year and I had exceeded that limit. The threshold was pretty low, allowing the bank to avoid most grassroots money laundering. But still, I was surprised.

When I talk about a Cash Buffer, it isn't actual notes and coins. It is money that you can easily access – and use – and it usually sits in an readily accessible bank account.

In Deloitte's 2022 survey of 14,000 Gen Z and Millennials around the world, they highlighted that 46 per cent of Gen Zs and 47 per cent of Millennials live pay-cheque to pay-cheque with no cash reserve. That's almost half the population aged between 20 and 40 who worry an unexpected expense will send them into debt and make them miss a bill payment. If you are in the same position, that kind of anxiety and dependence on your employer can be a heavy weight on your shoulders. You need a Cash

Buffer so you do not have to rely on expensive, sometimes dangerous, forms of debt or borrowing.

Most people find naming their Cash Buffer something meaningful helps maintain their motivation to save. You may prefer to call yours Freedom Money or My New Life Fund. I used to call mine The Fuck-Off Fund after reading an article called *The Story of a Fuck-Off Fund* by Paulette Perhach. The name sang to me. Whatever you call it, understand that having a Cash Buffer is a great step towards having financial flexibility and independence.

If you have other assets but no Cash Buffer, it could severely strain your financial resilience if you suddenly need to sell long-term investments (stocks or a residence) to cover your costs. It's not pretty, believe me. I have experienced a cash crunch where I needed to do this. The uncertainty of the sale and squeezed timeline was horrible. I received much less money from selling my investments under time pressure and in a falling market, and I was stressed all the time.

You may feel that your most immediate risk is losing your job. How long do you think you might be out of work? Three months? Six? Your Cash Buffer may help you move home so you can cut costs or find a different job, and cover you when you have no income.

An unexpected cost may come up – like a car repair or replacement – which is expensive and perhaps essential for you to work. Consider what insurance cover you have at your disposal. Is there an excess amount that you will need to pay first? Consider this in your Cash Buffer calculations.

The sweet spot is smaller than you think

My mistake was thinking I needed 12 months of income as a Cash Buffer – because, hell, that's what I had been told. It was such an astronomical amount of money to consider (after tax, too!) that I could not start saving. I didn't see the point since it would have taken me at least 25 years at my saving rate to get there. Not to mention the effects of inflation on any cash I held. It was 100 per cent a mental block. The number was too big, beyond anything I had considered possible. So I didn't even try.

Please, never let this be you. If three months of expenses seems too much to try to save, start small. Start with a week of costs and build from there. A week of breathing room is better than no breathing room at all. You can do it by putting something aside today.

According to research completed in 2021 by the Yorkshire Building Society, 19 per cent of UK adults have less than £100 in savings (meaning that more than ten million people had less than £100 in 2021).

If you have £100 or less in savings

What this says about you: You are not alone - more than 10m adults in the UK have less than £100 in savings.

What you can do now: Take an envelope (or a glass or a sock) and put a £1 coin away from where you keep your money. Add coins or notes as and when you can.

And also: Talk to a trusted family member about your situation if it is safe. Research what emergency support is available in your area.

More than £100 but less than £500

What this says about you: You are no longer a statistic but need more savings to reduce your worry about your finances and increase your confidence with money.

What you can do now: Focus on keeping the money flow one-way. It's much better to get into the habit of adding small amounts to your Cash Buffer and keeping them there. Avoid adding large amounts, only to withdraw the funds when you are short of money.

And also: Open a separate account where you can access your money, so there is a bit more friction. Keep adding to the account in small increments.

More than £500 but less than £2,000

What this says about you: You are now flexing your saving muscle and building your confidence about managing your money. You have a small and strengthening saving habit. You can now cover the cost of a replacement bicycle, car repair or MOT, or boiler repair. It may take time to replenish your buffer but you know you can do it.

What you can do now: You can start increasing your saving ability by a few more pounds each deposit.

And also: While you have a Cash Buffer for emergencies, prevention is better than cure. How about checking the air pressure in your car tires, taking note of any possible problems around your home, or upgrade your security lock for your bike.

More than £2,000 but less than £10,000

What this says about you: You hold a significant amount of money, which can cover a large unexpected expense.

What you can do now: Re-read Chapter 9 for more strategies about how to manage your expenses. Now you have more brain space to think, you can do more to improve your savings.

And also: Keep the one-way cashflow into the account as a golden rule. Set a goal for what you want your ideal Cash Buffer number to be.

More than £10,000

What this says about you: You now have enough money to cover a number of months of expenses.

What you can do now: Now is the time to look at what you have, and what you can do with it. This is not an invitation to spend your buffer, only to plan for the unexpected.

And also: You can now use your saving habit to build up an investment fund (and keep this Cash Buffer for emergencies).

A credit card is not an emergency fund

I have seen so-called money advisers or influencers who recommend keeping a credit card as a re-placement for an emergency fund. This is SO DAMN WRONG I have to shout it in capital letters.

Credit cards are expensive, and falling into the trap of using debt in an emergency will keep you indebted for a long time. When I last checked, credit cards charged upwards of 28 per cent per year for good credit. This means that you are trying desperately to repay the money before the interest is charged – you have no cash and are in expensive debt. You are trying to dig yourself out of a hole that keeps getting bigger. If you want to know how to use debt well – check out Chapter 12.

Why do influencers and advisors recommend credit cards? Because they are paid by the credit card companies to do so. Thankfully, you can usually tell when someone is being paid by a credit card company because they will usually name-check the brand, or there will be a disclosure at the end of the relevant blog, post or article. But use your head – if someone is trying to convince you to use a credit card, you are being sold a product. It is another form of advertising. Avoid it like the plague.

Automate your savings

Wherever possible, use automated payments to top up your savings. Having a separate account, sub-account or savings bucket which you don't look at every day is vital. You know it's there in the background, but the temptation to take from it is reduced because you don't see it. Out of sight, out of mind. Or, you could think of it this way: it is much easier to resist buying a cake if you are not at the shop counter looking at it all the time.

As interest rates climb, you could take advantage of banking products that will reward you with higher interest rates the longer you keep money in the account. Ensure you can access the funds without additional penalties in an emergency. The ideal way to automate your savings is to time the withdrawal as soon as you are paid – that way, you are less likely to feel the loss of the saved amount. After a while it simply becomes another transfer in the many transactions in your account.

How much is enough for you?

Ten thousand pounds is a pretty arbitrary number, covering at least two to three months' living expenses for most households in the UK. But you may think it might not last long if you are out of work for more than a few months.

This is where you need to sit down and ask yourself the following questions. Write down as many details as you possibly can:

- How long have I been out of work in the past?

- What effect did that have on me, my mental health and my motivation to work?

- Have I ever been surprised at how long it has taken to find a new job?

- Have I ever lived through an economic downturn and what did I learn from it? If not, what might my work prospects be like in the next one?

- What can I anticipate?

- Apart from my Cash Buffer, what other forms of support do I have around me? Are there family members who I can call on for help?

- How important is it for me to remain independent?

- Am I worrying too much or too little about a lack of income?

- What are my strengths when it comes to solving problems?

- What is my current income in comparison to the market? Am I overpaid or underpaid? What effect will this have on my expectations and employability?

- Do I want to take more than two to three months off if I am suddenly without paid work?

- Would a sabbatical or a mental break from paid work be worthwhile? What would the pros and cons be? How long do I need, or want?

- Am I currently living up to the level of my income?

- Are there changes I am willing to make (for example, clothing, eating out, subscriptions) when I am not in paid work? What could they be?

- What is holding me back from reducing my

expenditure now? What pressures do I have to spend money?

- Is there any way I can reduce them? What insurance cover do I have?

- Are there excess payments to be made if something goes wrong?

You may also want to consider what might happen if there is a medical emergency – yours or a loved one's.

- Who in my life may have a medical emergency?

- What is that likely to be?

- Will I need to travel?

- How much could that cost in time and money?

- Will I need to take time off work and for how long?

- What kind of support will I want to give?

- What might be the follow-on impact?

- Will I need to provide ongoing support?

- Will I need ongoing support myself?

Focus on your expenses, not your income

Building a replacement income through your Cash Buffer
can be daunting and could be a long-term project. I
encourage you to look at your outgoings and start by
building several months of living costs first, rather than
trying to replace your income. Only spending money
on essential expenses – otherwise known as extreme
frugality – can be stressful and lead to burnout. However,
it is helpful to know what you could survive on for a
little while if you stripped out all the optional extras
from your spending. Take a quick note of your immediate
household expenses, including: housing costs; utilities;
council tax; mobile phone and internet costs; food;
schooling; essential clothing; medicine and hygiene; and
transport. What is the total?

A typical basic budget for a month might look like the
following example.

Housing £1,400
Utilities and Council tax £400
Phone and internet £35
Food £400
Medicine £20
Transport £100
Total: £2,255

There is absolutely no fun factored in here, no socialising nor entertainment. No gym subscriptions. No haircuts or self-care. This is not how I recommend living because it is stressful and demoralising. But it does demonstrate how easy it is to spend that extra disposable income.

Perhaps it helps to look at your Cash Buffer in terms of how many months of essentials can you cover versus how many months of income? For example:

> **Your current Cash Buffer:** £5,000
> **Your current income (monthly, after tax etc.):** £4,000
> **Your current spend on essentials:** £2,255
> **Your Cash Buffer covers:** 1.2 months of income or 2.2 months of expenses

When you slow down your rate of spending, it can make a huge difference to how long your Cash Buffer will last.

How much cash do you need?

This is difficult to assess and you are the only person who can answer that question. But these are my steps for working out what you need:

- Look at your monthly spending (not your income).

- See where you can trim a few expenses.

- Imagine your most likely risk – an expensive car repair or loss of a job – and work out how much it will cost you. It could be three months of expenses or the cost of another vehicle (and registration, taxes, etc.).

- Add in a cushion so you feel comfortable with this amount and you can make the odd mistake.

- Modify and adjust (adjust down to make it achievable, adjust up to feel more secure).

- Revisit this amount when your life circumstances change.

The Life of a Cash Buffer

Here is another way of looking at your Cash Buffer: it grows and changes. Just because it's small now, doesn't mean it won't get bigger. Having some sort of visual reference for your mind's eye can help you maintain focus and motivation to add to your Cash Buffer. Take a look at the pictures of these frogs below and check where you are now on the Froggy Cash Buffer Scale. Now you know where you are visually, what's the next step you can take up the scale?

Pre-tadpole phase: Amounts don't matter here. Build the habit of saving. If you are starting from zero, what is an amount that you can put aside each day or each week without fail?

Tadpole phase: Now is the time to put a number on your regular saving habit. Start small. I recommend less than £10 each time. The important thing is frequency – how often will you save this amount? Daily? Weekly? Make it as often as possible. If you can, set up a regular savings account which rewards you for keeping your money untouched with higher interest rates.

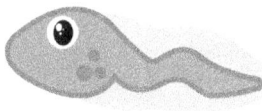

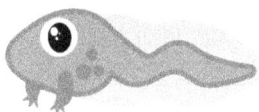

Sprog phase: You are getting good at this. What does your Cash Buffer cover right now? What emergency would you like it to cover in the future? How much will that be? How often can you save towards it? How much can you put aside each time? Now is the time to put that money into a higher-interest savings account to encourage you to keep it in one spot and not touch it.

Frog phase: You have at least a month's expenses and are ahead of the game! As you look elsewhere to make your money work (for example, investments) – can you maintain your saving habit? Of course, you can! Keep the amounts achievable and the frequency at least once a month.

Frog Prince(ss) phase: Well done you – this is great stuff! How many months' expenses do you need? Saving can be addictive, but remember that you must put your money to work one day. Assess how much you have available and what you need to feel like you have plenty of choices and financial flexibility.

Priya's Frog Scale Cash Buffer

Priya, a freelancer (42), is paid every two weeks on Wednesday mornings. The amounts are up and down, but the schedule is pretty reliable.

"I have £500 saved already , which puts me in the Sprog phase of saving. I can cover most car expenses if I need to - but not much else. I want to reach the Frog phase,

*which means one month of expenses. I will put money
aside every two weeks on Wednesday - as soon as I see
the money arrive in my account. Usually, I check when
I'm eating breakfast. I will put 5 per cent aside each time
because it seems small enough to be achievable and I
won't notice it so much.*

*"The money will go into a Regular Saver account with my
bank. It lets me save up to £250 per month and pays
a reasonable interest rate (if I keep my money there). A
month's expenses will be about £2,500 for me. At this rate
I think I will take me ten months to top my buffer up to a
full £2,500 if I save on average £100 every two weeks.*

*"Perhaps I could go a bit faster – but this is definitely
within reach. This is important because I was sick last
year and couldn't work for a month. It was so stressful
and I struggled to recover from the experience. I am now
anxious about falling sick again; it is impacting my life. I
don't want to worry about being sick again. I want my joie
de vivre back."*

Exercise – Name Your Cash Buffer

If the words Cash Buffer don't fill your heart with flutters
of anticipation – you need to find a different name for your
fund that will motivate you. Think about what is important
to you? What do you wish for which seems out of reach?
Remember, your Cash Buffer isn't there to be spent.

Instead, what it buys you is so much more important than an instant spending zing. It is the freedom to choose your career path. It is the calmness to have a stress-free week. It is the knowledge that your car can break down - but you won't. It is the ability to drop everything and help your loved ones if something goes suddenly wrong.

Take a few minutes to think of what is important to you and write down at least ten ideas of what you could name your Cash Buffer.

1.

2.

3.

4.

5.

6.

7.

8.

9.

10.

Once you have your possibilities down on paper, complete the following sentence with each of the names.

My [Cash Buffer name] is important to me because [say why it is important to you here].

For example:

"My Fuck-Off Fund is important to me because I want to work for an ethical company."

"My Emergency Fund is important to me because I want to shield my children from money worries."

Say this out loud each time and listen to yourself. Is there one statement or name that really means something to you? Is there a name that stands out? Choose the one that moves you emotionally and use it to refer to your financial life preserver.

Exercise – Right-Size Your Cash Buffer and Make the Habit Stick

To start or maintain a new habit, it is essential to write down as many details about how, when, where and what will trigger you to do the thing. Let's get you started.

Write down how much you have saved
already. Amount:

Where does this amount put you on the Frog
Prince(ss) scale? Tadpole / Sprog / Frog / Frog
Princess

What is the next step on the Frog Prince(ss)
scale? Tadpole / Sprog / Frog / Frog Princess

How regularly will you put money aside?
Daily / Weekly / Fortnightly / Monthly on the
following date:

Which day(s) of the week will you put the
money aside? Day(s):

Where will you put the money? Location:

How much are you saving each time?
Amount:

When do you calculate you can achieve your
goal? Date:

Why is this important to you? Your reason:

Start Right Now!

Starting any new endeavour can be daunting. If you are
overwhelmed by thinking about your ultimate goal, it
can hold you back from starting - as I found out to my
disappointment. However, I can guarantee that you will
look back on life in ten years, and think with incredulity
about how energetic and youthful you are now. You have
the energy and capability that you need within you.

Check your response about your Cash Buffer on the
Money Pizza in Chapter 1. How do you feel about your
Cash Buffer now – more positive? Even if you have no Cash
Buffer, can you picture a way to get started?

THIS CHAPTER CAN BE revisited whenever you feel your motivation to save ebbing away. Life changes all the time and what motivates you will change as well. Your needs will shift and your financial life preserver will also adjust. Now that you know what you need to do, it will be easier to repeat.

If you are 40-plus and think you are too old to start building a life preserver, what will your 60-year-old self say to you? It will be urging you to take the opportunity today. You do have the know-how to start. Look at the small step in front of you and take that step. And just keep going at your own pace.

Chapter Eleven

Strategic Investments

"The four most dangerous words in investing are, it's different this time."

Sir John Templeton

C HANCES ARE YOU ALREADY have ideas about what you would like to invest in. I believe many people are naturally comfortable and suited to certain types of investment and I struggle with blanket rules about investment strategies. It really depends on you and your circumstances. However, when it comes to risky assets and strategies (or financial products which I don't consider investments) – I have a simple rule. I'll share it with you below to help you scratch that trading itch.

This chapter does not focus on the investment products themselves – there are too many to consider – but how to make well thought out investment decisions. By the end of this chapter you will have a better idea about what you consider an investment, as well as some spending ideas which are definitely not investments; understand how to shield yourself from the hype around investments; and have a framework of questions to ask yourself for every and any investment decision you make.

My investment mantra is: *"Never confuse entertainment with investments. Entertainment should never be predictable and boring; and investments should always be predictable and boring."*

What is an investment

My own definition of an investment, which has stood the test of a changing lifestyle, is:

> *"Something I can put time or money into, which can be a reliable or predictable store of value, a source of income, or an effective offset to a cost I have."*

Does 'reliable or predictable' bring to mind images of dull and practical people or things? A bit of a yawn and a stretch? Good. That is exactly what you are aiming for with your investments.

An investment instrument could be anything, from: buying a bundle of shares; units in a fund; a loan; a business; bonds; angel investments; a house; a rental property; or commercial property.

Also, consider your own education and self-development as an investment. While it costs you time and money, it can increase your income in the longer term when you put it to good use.

When making a personal investment decision, you won't need to look at the whole investment universe (in fact, it's impossible to do so). It may help you to know that even in the investment industry, while there are many models which can be used to analyse various investments, decision makers have a limited scope and often have to rely on their own knowledge to make the investment choice.

At school, university or business school you may be taught tools to choose and compare investments, including: return on investment; return on equity; weighted average cost of capital; or payback period. I could go on and on.

In real life, it is rare to have two investment opportunities come up at the same time, with the same information, which you can compare perfectly. And there's the rub. Textbooks teach how to make a decision with perfect information and complete detachment. In reality you have imperfect information and you will be very emotionally invested in where your money goes. Such a decision can be far harder than any exam question presented with perfect information.

When making a business decision, funds may not be the limiting factor (happy days – it's somebody else's dime!) so your choices can be made in terms of 'return'. But personally, your choice is more likely to be limited by affordability.

The groundwork

Answering the question, 'What should I invest in?' can be as complicated or as straightforward as you want it to be. Because of this ambiguity, the wealth of information (pardon the pun) and competing opinions on where to put your money can be hard to sift through. Chances are you have one big investment in mind right now (it could be buying real estate or spending time and money retraining) or maybe something in the future (preparing for retirement).

It is useful to define your proposed investment with what I call an Investment Framework, which defines the parameters of the investment you want. This means you can:

- test if what you want is reasonable;

- find which investment instrument(s) fits your framework;

- evaluate what fits, and choose your investment; and

- re-evaluate your investment (when the time comes).

This also gives you what professionals call 'a bit of rigour' to your investment decision. If you are constantly trying to tweak your investment requirements – ask yourself, 'Why?' Are the requirements too rigid? Too limited? Does your investment theory suck? Is your investment theory awesome, but the instrument doesn't exist yet? Do you need to change your ideas?

Don't worry if this seems overwhelming, we will go through the Investment Framework in more detail below.

What is not an investment

There are so many big-ticket items people like to call investments but they are not. Let's have a look at some of these. The following are all items that sophisticated investors (ahem, rich people) have tried to convince me are good 'investments':

- Holiday time shares

- A Birkin Bag

- Jewellery and watches

- Wine

- Artworks and Non-Fungible Tokens (otherwise known as NFTs)

- Cars, motorbikes, bicycles and boats

- Clothing

- Cryptocurrencies

In fact, at one point or another, each of the items above have been marketed directly to me as an 'investment' (and I use the inverted quotes deliberately here). Perhaps the same thing has happened to you. 'Buy this statement fashion piece! It will be an investment in your wardrobe!' You hear messages like this all the time.

You may laugh – but stop for a moment and think about how some people defend or justify spending money on these listed items. Phrases like, 'It's an investment in myself' are much easier to trot out rather than, 'I've had a rubbish day, and I'm feeling fat, so I've decided that a nice new dress will make me feel better'. 'Wine is a great investment' is better than saying, 'I really want to demonstrate to you how much spare money I have that I can literally afford to drink it in my spare time. I'm that successful, ya'see.'

New cars lose their value as soon as you drive them out of the car park and a vintage car may only hold its value if it is extremely rare (or there is some other cashed up enthusiast out there bidding up the price). A big reason you buy a vintage car is to flag that you are successful enough to sink money and time into an old machine. That is not an investment, it is an expensive hobby.

Some cars and other vehicles may offset your transport costs, but unless you are buying an inexpensive second-hand model which is very reliable, you may not be effectively offsetting those costs. More likely you will increase your transport expenses for the sake of comfort, speed and having a vehicle which looks good. And boats are never, ever a good investment. They are big enjoyable toys to sink your money into. Ditto for house boats, unless you live on them full time.

You may ask why I include cryptocurrencies and NFTs in the 'not-an-investment' bucket. Fundamentally, these are both based on a new technology and they are subject to the whims of market fluctuations. Cryptocurrencies are not regulated and neither are the exchanges upon which they are traded. It is completely a matter of trust whether you are buying what you think you are buying and for that I consider cryptocurrencies a gamble (at best) and a fraud (at worst).

True, some of the items I list above may hold their value, and some may go up in value. Sometimes. However for most, their future value will either diminish or be determined by the whims of fashion and popularity. The luxury industry has grown very well by convincing wealthy people certain consumables are investments. Most of the items in the list above do not reliably store value and they don't provide income. They are simply expensive (but rather nice) ways to spend money (and to tell the world that you have money to spend). I want to talk about investing. Spending money on the things above is ... spending money.

Don'ts and dos of investing

Don'ts

Analysis paralysis: you can always gather more information and build another spreadsheet. At some point you have to stop thinking and make a bloody decision!

Doing nothing: you have decided. But it's a worthless decision until you do something.

Investing in only one thing (or type of thing): don't put all your eggs in one basket. Diversify your investments! Bought a home? Great! If you live in the UK, start an ISA (Individual Savings Account).

Trying to cheat the tax man: "I don't have to declare this." Hmmm, nup! One day that clever loophole might close and you may have a whacking big tax bill.

Sophisticated strategies: Collateralised loan obligations? Swaps? Options? Unless this is your area of expertise, do not go near complex sounding products. Only invest in what you understand. If this is your profession, invest in the boring stuff first.

Expensive shit or upsizing your investment: this is particularly relevant to real estate investments. Never max out all your resources in one investment. Do you need a luxury new-build? Really? Do you really need a guest room? What if the value of your investment goes down? Think twice about how much you are sinking into the investment.

Stuff you wouldn't buy for yourself: this is very relevant to your first real estate purchase. If you wouldn't live in it, don't buy it. One day, you may have to live in it.

Get rich quick: if it sounds like the best idea ever (!) it is probably someone trying to cheat you.

Doing it all yourself: sometimes a 5 per cent fee is cheap and free brokerage is expensive. How much is your time worth? Good investment managers and tax accountants can provide an effective time offset. They can help you ask the right questions. If you have complex tax arrangements, it is worth hiring someone who will ensure your tax is right. Unless of course, you are a tax accountant. In that case, do your own tax return!

Dos

Be an imperfect investor: investing in a 'good enough' investment now, is better than waiting too long for the 'perfect investment' to appear.

Invest in the boring stuff first: pension savings and tax-free ISA accounts.

Keep it understandable: if you can't explain it over (or after) a glass of wine, perhaps it isn't the best investment for you.

Decide: then act.

Bonus: time value of money

If you have spare time and don't know about it already, learn about this term right now. Seriously, it is all you will ever need to know to understand what your money is doing as time goes by. Some people say you should do this first ... enough to get started. Learning about the Time Value of Money can take time and effort and could send you down the rabbit hole of investment theory. But understanding the time value of money is the path to financial literacy and independence. Learn this, apply your knowledge, and nobody will be able to bullshit you again. Go on, chuck 'time value of money' at your search engine and see what pops out.

The two per cent rule

Remember how I said you could still scratch that trading itch? I understand people find it interesting to pick stocks and actively invest in speculative trades without thinking through all the details of what the investment really means. Other people wish to invest in the 'next big thing' (including NFTs and crypto) because they like the buzz. If this is you, I'm not going to say, 'Change your ways, sinner!' but I am going to give you my best advice.

Always keep these speculative, exciting, trades to no more than two per cent of your net wealth. If you lose your money, you will be able to absorb your mistake. And never – ever – use leverage (otherwise known as debt) to enhance your two per cent risky investment pot. If you do this, it is gambling – pure and simple.

An eight-point investment framework

The following investment framework can help you test an idea, and collect relevant information to help you make a well thought out investment decision. You can then revisit and re-evaluate it as many times as you like in the future. There are eight key topics to think about when considering any investment. These form the investment framework.

1. What is the point of making this investment?

Sometimes this question is overlooked – but it is an important consideration. If you find you want to invest because you find the instrument interesting or exciting, or everyone else is doing it – please look at my two per cent rule.

You might wish to invest to:

- generate a secondary income;

- make a capital gain or to save money;

- offset or otherwise manage a cost;

- insure against a future loss (of job, health etc);

- save towards the day that you don't have to work for a living.

Your reason may not be on the list above, but it is critically important to consider and to write it down.

2. What do you want to invest in?

ISAs: adults in the UK can invest up to £20,000 per year in an Individual Savings Account and all income and capital gain (increase in value) from those investments remain tax fee. You can invest in stocks, shares, bonds and other pooled investments (funds) for diversification.

Pension or private retirement savings: you can make pre-tax contributions to defined contribution pension schemes, which can be tax effective because you are likely to be at a lower tax rate once you retire and draw your pension.

Property: most people want to own their own home or some form of property. In an uncertain or flat market (as we are currently experiencing), capital gains are unlikely or limited. However, a mortgage payment may be an effective substitute to a rental cost. Alternatively, you may be able to earn rental income on the property, which could offset your own housing costs.

A side hustle: do you have time, spare cash and the inclination to start a micro-business?

Insurance: health insurance, life insurance, mortgage insurance, house and contents insurance etc. Are you adequately covered? Is your family adequately covered if you suddenly become unable to earn money? Conversely, are you over-insured?

A small or a big business: which can generate ongoing income, or be sold in the future to make a capital gain (or, if you are skilful, both).

If your investment falls outside this brief list, you need to consider closely whether or not it can be considered an actual investment which will deliver the value you require. It may well do, but you need to analyse it carefully. As an aside – I consider education an investment, too.

3. Where is the investment?

Work out your geographic focus. A global strategy is not a focus. Where is your investment going to be?

- In the UK/EU/overseas?

- Home or locally (if they are different locations). Near family or away? Near work? What if your work situation changes?

- Where is your country of tax residence? Are there any tax advantages associated with it?

- Are there legal or tax advantages of investing in certain areas?

- Do you have local knowledge? (You grew up there, or you lived there for more than ten years and can speak the language fluently.)

- Will you be investing in a currency that is different to where you earn your money?

- Could a changing exchange rate cause problems?

4. Stump up the money

How will you fund your investment and, perhaps more importantly, how much can you afford to spend? It is likely that you will use one, or a combination, of the following:

- bank loan, or a non-banking institution loan;

- private loan (including the bank of Mum and Dad);

- Limited Partnership;

- shareholders with funding capital (ordinary

shares, preference shares etc);

- after tax rental income from the investment itself;

- profit or capital gain from the investment itself;

- your salary/income;

- cash or savings.

Once you know how you are going to fund your intended investment, add up the pounds and work out how much you can afford to spend (a) up front; and (b) on an ongoing basis.

5. How much will my funding cost? When do I have to pay it back?

Will you have the cash to pay for this investment or are you borrowing money from elsewhere? Make sure your cashflows match up. For example, receiving dividends quarterly will not help if your debt repayments are every month.

Does the bank of Mum and Dad have a 0 per cent interest rate? (It's worth asking.) When do they want to be paid back?

What does a bank loan cost? What are the fees and interest rate? Will the cost change in the future? Can you cover the payments as and when they are due? How?

Can you repay the money bit-by-bit, or must it be in one lump sum on a date in the future?

Can you make over-payments at your own option? This can save you interest costs, but be aware fees for overpayment might apply.

Do you have investors who require the assets to be liquidated and money to be returned in a certain period of time?

Can your investors make calls on their money (ask for it back) at any time?

Remember, if you have self-funded your investment, you do not have to pay - or answer to - anyone else.

6. Timeline and exit strategy

Are you one of those people who enters planes and always checks the exits (especially if they are behind you)? I am. And I do the same thing when making investment decisions. Firstly, I think about what I am investing for and secondly, when I need withdraw the money from my investments.

Always consider the following questions before making your investment.

- Are you saving for retirement (decades)?

- Do you want to sell up in three years or more?

- How easy to sell is your asset and how big is the market (stocks versus real estate versus private businesses)?

- When do you need to repay your funding? Will you do this from a sale of the asset or bit-by-bit?

- How will you achieve a sale (private sale, listing, auction, stop loss order)? When is that likely to happen? Does this line up with how your investors need to be repaid?

Can you sell (liquidate) your asset easily? Just because something is easy to buy – it doesn't necessarily mean it's easy to sell. Many investment companies have established platforms where it's easy to buy into investment trusts (an investment managed by someone else on your behalf). But when it comes time to sell, it's much more difficult than you think.

Do not be fooled into assuming that because it was quick and easy for you to buy – especially if you bought it using your smartphone – that you can sell as fast. The same thing goes for investments in properties. If you have gone through the process of buying your own property easily as the buyer, remember next time you will be the seller and it may take a while for the right buyer at the right price to come along.

The most liquid assets are those that are traded on an exchange – and this is usually a stock exchange – because the purpose of the exchange is precisely to bring pools of buyers and sellers together.

7. Investment Structure: how will you invest?

Always consider the following aspects before making your investment. Will you invest:

- In your own name? Your partner's? Parents'?

- For your company?

- Through a trust?

- Through a managed fund?

- On a stock market?

- In real estate (leasehold versus freehold)?

- In funds?

- In a private venture?

- In a special purpose vehicle?

8. Taking care of the investment: who will manage it?

I love investments that are mostly 'set and forget'. Consider the cost; level of capability; and your trust in whoever may be managing your investments, including yourself. Managers can be any of the following:

- Real estate agents and managers

- Fund managers

- Stock brokers

- Employees

- Your partner

- Yourself

If you have noted down your requirements in each of these eight areas, you now have a basic investment framework to refer to. Risk is not included as a separate field in this framework because the questions above help you evaluate certain scopes without labelling them as a risk. Being absolutely clear about your funding costs, timelines, and exit strategies will help focus your mind on possible cash flow shortages. All the investments mentioned above involve a reasonable amount of risk and the longer the timeline you have, the more risk you can tolerate.

If you find in your personal life (or indeed, in your professional life), big decisions are being made without these questions being asked, it's up to you to ask them.

Exercise – Your Investment Framework

Take a piece of paper and using as much detail and hard facts as possible, answer each of these questions in relation to the investment you are considering:

1. What is prompting you to make this investment? What do you want to get out of it (Income? Housing? Capital gains)?

2. What are you investing in? Does it appear on the 'Not an investment' list?

3. Where will the investment be? What are the pros and cons of the location?

4. How is the investment funded? How much will your funding cost? Can you afford it?

5. Where is the money coming from to make this investment and when does it have to be repaid?

6. What is your investment timeline and exit strategy?

7. How will you make the investment, directly or indirectly?

8. Who will manage the investment and take care of it in the longer term?

P HEW – YOU MADE it! This is an important chapter. If you feel a little overwhelmed, put the book down and come back to it in a couple of weeks. It's pretty chunky stuff, and may take some time to process. For now, check back on your answer to the Investments slice of the Money Pizza in Chapter 1. Is there anything you want to reassess?

Reconsider the investment framework each time you are making an investment decision. It may seem like a lot of work and it is. But your investments, your money and your livelihood are so important. It is worth putting this work in first.

Making great investment decisions and managing them well requires consistent attention. Understand that your life and goals change and your investments will need to change too.

Congratulations for making it this far and considering all of this information. You should now feel more confident in your ability to make great investment decisions and to recognise where you may need to seek extra help and advice from knowledgeable professionals. Trust yourself and your ability to ask informed questions. The answers you receive will help you fill out your investment framework and clarify your decision.

Now you have the capability and tools to make the right investment decisions for yourself. Bravo!

CHAPTER TWELVE

How to Use Debt Wisely

"Ten million dollars after I'd become a star, I was deeply in debt."

Sammy Davis, Jr.

THIS CHAPTER IS ABOUT debt – but don't let that put you off! Keep reading. Used prudently, debt can be a valuable tool in your financial life. However, you may become a slave to your debt when you use it without understanding it. We will go through the pros and cons of using debt and what I call the 'good, bad and ugly' of debt products.

By the end of this chapter, you will have enough knowledge to look at your attitude to debt, what obligations you may already have and what type they are. You will have tips about how to avoid too much debt and why it is essential to ensure you are reading the correct information. Finally, if you are struggling with debt, I give you my best pointers about what to do and where to find trustworthy help.

Debt is neither all good nor all bad … but that will not stop me from having a good old rant about how debt is peddled, advertised and pushed onto people. It's up to you to be thoughtful when you consider debt. If you think debt is 100 per cent bad, you may cut yourself off from the opportunity to purchase a valuable asset. However, if you think debt is 100 per cent fine, you will likely be in deep trouble very quickly.

Pros and cons of using debt

- It can help you buy a significant asset when you have little to no income (for example, if you need to pay for tertiary education).

- Almost everyone buying their own home will use a mortgage, which is a long-term form of debt.

- Many people use debt like forced savings. They know they will retain the discipline of repaying the debt on time because of the consequences if they do not.

- However, many forms of debt are costly, including: credit cards; car leases; and personal loans.

- Debt can be complex to understand.

- Using debt to buy consumables (clothes, food, technology etc.) or items that depreciate quickly (cars) can be disastrous because you are left with a valueless item and an expensive debt.

- Due to the compounding effect of interest, if you do not keep up with your payments, they will increase and may lead to bankruptcy if you cannot pay your debts.

I propose a mid-way in using debt, including: be careful with it; understand your debt; and don't let it control you. The best time to understand debt is before you borrow the money – but the second-best time is now. Understanding what you have already is a significant step to managing your debt well.

Arianna's debt lesson story

Arianna (24) comes from an Italian family that places a lot of importance on never using debt or credit cards. After leaving school, she managed her money well and held down jobs through university.

"I haven't told my parents that I have a student loan – they think it's a grant from the government and that I won't have to pay back the money. I'm okay with the student loan myself, it's with the government, and I only need to pay it back from a percentage of my income once I'm

earning enough. Honestly, I haven't looked at it and don't even know the interest rate.

"I want to start my own business, and I have no money for the necessary equipment. Mum and Dad have been great in teaching me discipline with money – but now I need a loan, and I'm terrified! I have a vague idea about interest rates, but when it comes down to it, I'm too scared to find out what is on offer. I don't even know if I would be able to pay back the loan. It's stopping me from going to a bank to find out more. All the information seems confusing."

Debt: the good

Debt is not all bad. But it needs to be understood and managed well. I consider debt to be good if it has the following features:

- It is used to purchase an asset which provides future income or housing (for example, education leading to long-term, satisfying employment, or a home).

- The interest rate is low – between 0.5 and 7 per cent.

- The repayments are a manageable percentage of your income – ideally less than 25 per cent of your take-home pay.

- You can enjoy the benefits of your purchase indefinitely.

You might notice the features of good debt are as much about what you buy with it as the debt it-self. It's the asset underneath that is important.

Remember too much of a good thing can be terrible. Resist the urge to buy more than you need – especially when it comes to housing – just because someone will give you a loan. If you have too much mortgage debt, it will be a burden on your life and reduce your financial flexibility. Understand that house envy never ends – we almost always want more than we have. Do not use debt to feed your house envy otherwise it will become out of control.

I count personal and business loans as good debt when you use these loans to purchase assets (perhaps a necessary vehicle) or to start or grow your business. While many banks are maligned, I still recommend obtaining these loans from banks or credit unions, and not from other non-bank debt providers. At the time of writing, these non-bank loans are starting to look expensive, at more than 10 per cent per year. That means for every £1,000 you borrow, you need to pay an extra £100 each year.

Personal and business loans have the benefit of being smaller (between £1,000-£50,000) than a massive mortgage and are often flexible in how you repay them.

But the interest rate can go up if base rates go up, which can become very expensive. Consider if you might be better off saving up instead of borrowing this money.

Whether you consider the debt good or not – my advice is to never buy what you don't need with debt.

Student Debt

Society now expects teenagers to go to university as a step in their career path, but many people do so without considering their degree's value. Look at how secondary schools market themselves, and you will realise this puts fundamental and unspoken pressure on all school-aged people that the preferred progression after school is university. There are many useless university degrees out there. All they do is allow you to spend three or four expensive years living on campus trying to figure out what you want to do with your life.

I can say this because – yes – this is what I did. I went straight to university from school, not very interested in my engineering degree. Unsurprisingly, I partied a lot, studied very little and dropped out at the start of the third year. I had to have a severe re-think about what I wanted to do with my life and start making real decisions. Ultimately, I switched degrees, graduated from another university and finally secured a real job. However, I had about AU$84,000 in student debt, which I paid via two per cent taken out of my salary each month.

For one reason or another, I decided to clear the debt so it would no longer clock up interest. I hated the idea of being in debt. I made extra payments each year to decrease it to a more manageable sum. Finally, I received a small inheritance from my grandmother and used that to pay down the last of my outstanding debt. I remember the day clearly – the mix of relief at having cleared that debt – and the regret I wasn't using that inheritance to build anything new with my grandmother's legacy.

With the benefit of hindsight, I would have been much better off taking a year or two out of school and working in a pub or as a sports coach for a while before making a hurried decision to go to university. Those three years of bumbling about on campus were fun and educational (in their way) but very expensive. I estimate I spent AU$42,000 on wasted tuition fees alone (I also failed a subject or two). Looking back – it was a total waste of money.

My advice to my younger self is, buck the expectation that you need to go to university straight away. Spend time doing those boring jobs (working at a pub, teaching snotty kids how to row, working in a pen factory) first. Think, really think, about what it is that could make you happy in the longer term. Get away from the scoreboard of school and achievement and give your poor brain a rest. Start saving money.

Debt: the bad

I'm not fond of credit cards. For one thing, they should be named something else because you are not receiving credit (which implies free cash); you are taking out expensive debt. Let's label them 'very expensive debt cards' to call them what they actually are. Unfortunately, very-expensive debt cards look almost exactly like debit cards (which use your actual money).

Very expensive debt cards entice users with promises of loyalty rewards and travel points, which is why I have one. But if you don't pay your expensive debt balance in full each month, you can be charged a whopping 28 per cent or more. Buy now, pay later providers operate in much the same way. Once any interest-free period passes, the outstanding balance clocks up interest in the same way a card balance will.

Unlike a mortgage, where your home could be repossessed if you don't keep up your payments, very expensive debt cards are usually unsecured. That means the company lending you money doesn't have a right to take back the items you bought with the debt. On the other hand, a bank can repossess your home if you don't keep up with mortgage payments. This doesn't mean that you can ignore the unsecured debt, however. Missing payments on your very-expensive debt card will negatively affect your credit score, which may prevent you from benefiting from less expensive loans or even being able to obtain a rental agreement. In addition, your debt may be sold onto a debt purchaser who will actively and aggressively pursue the debt.

Very-expensive debt cards and buy-now-pay-later do nothing but encourage you to spend more and more and more. Often this is how people start on the slide of accumulating problem debt. They become hooked on the feeling and image of being able to buy things now without having to wait. The consequences of overconsumption like this are harmful to you and the planet.

Frank's credit card story

A naturally prudent person, Frank (31) was proud of the way he had managed his money. Until he had his first credit card. But it was only years later that he realised the mistake he had made in not understanding what he was getting himself into.

"I've never considered myself a lavish spender – so never identified with the stereotypical image of a shop-a-holic. I had taken out a credit card because I was told it would help me build my credit score, and I thought I could use it in case I had an emergency. I didn't think my limit was very high because I asked the bank for their lowest limit possible. They gave me a card with a £10,000 credit limit, and it was connected to my bank account.

"One day, I had that emergency that I had been anticipating, and I found myself putting £3,000 in costs on the card all at once. I felt relieved that I could do it, and told myself that I would pay attention to the credit card bills when they came in. It was one purchase only and I thought I would be fine.

"Life became stressful, and I struggled to keep on top of the day to day tasks I had to do. But I made sure I opened up my credit card bill and paid the minimum payment which was printed at the top of my statement. I didn't have the time or the headspace to do anything more.

"I don't really want to go into details – but this continued for months. Life was stressful and I was just staying on top of things. It was hard work. After about a year and a half, I was in a better place mentally. I thought I would check how much was left to pay off on my credit card to see if I could clear the final bit.

"I thought I would only have a fraction of the initial £3,000 left to pay because I had not missed a payment. To my surprise, I had more than £3,200 due on my credit card. How could that be? I asked myself. That's impossible! I turns out that I didn't understand my credit card at all. The interest rate was more than 30 per cent and they charged an annual fee. It took me another year to clear the debt and it was really hard work. In the end, I worked out I had paid more than £5,000 to the credit

card company in total. More than £2,000 in interest. All
because I didn't understand how the interest rate, fees
and repayment worked. I felt so stupid."

Credit card debt is pretty bad, but not as bad as it could
be.

Debt: the ugly

Apart from high interest loans from loan sharks, I believe
the worst kind of debt is car financing. It's expensive; it
encourages you to buy a car you don't need; it has inbuilt
upsells; and your car could be repossessed. But the worst
thing, the very worst thing, is ... you don't even own the
car at the end of the loan period.

In reality, car financing is a costly form of car rental, but
you still have the responsibility for registration, upkeep
and vehicle insurance.

The most financially detrimental thing you could do is
acquire the use of a brand-new car with financing. If you
drive that baby off the plot, it will have lost 25 per cent
of its value before the new car smell has faded. But you
often end up paying 15 per cent to 20 per cent per year
in interest on the sticker cost of the car. How is that for
adding insult to injury?

Roberto's car finance story

Roberto is 42 and a father-to-be. Having moved countries, he has no credit history. His wife is seven months pregnant and she explained in clear tones that she was not going to walk in the February snow to deliver the baby at the hospital. Neither would she wait for a taxi or ambulance if it came to that, thank-you-very-much. They decided they needed a bog-standard family car to drive around and so Roberto can easily reach his clients in other cities.

> *"I don't need a fancy car, but I need a car. I know what I want, and a Ford dealership is up the street. We have spent all our cash moving city and setting up the new place, so I don't have much (if anything) for a deposit on a car. Without a credit history here, it's problematic securing a personal loan. Car financing seems to be the way to go. The monthly payments are manageable at £125 per month and it helps me build a credit history. My wife is the banker, and she doesn't like the lease terms but right now, she has other things on her mind."*

Fast forward three years, Roberto and his wife have a toddler, and the three-year term is coming up on the car. Roberto wants to upgrade the car, so they have a built-in GPS, a USB adapter, and a few other features. His credit score is perfect, thanks to his payment record and given that the car looks a bit shabby, he wouldn't mind an upgrade in trim. The dealership offers him a newer model, with only a modest increase in payments (£160 per month) and a small down payment of £1,000. It seems like a good deal. He has saved up about £4,000 in emergency cash and can easily pay it.

But he told me,

> *"My wife asked to look at the lease terms and almost had a fit. I thought the dealership was offering me a better deal on a better car because of my good credit history. But it turned out there were some nasty elements. At the end of the term, I still wouldn't own the car. I would have to give it back. I knew the car could be repossessed, but I always thought of it as mine when it wasn't.*

> *"With the upgrade, they weren't giving me a better deal either. The interest rate would increase from 12.5 per cent to 15 per cent per year – but they hid that behind the payments which were always quoted in pounds per month. Then, the term increased from three to five years, locking me in for a longer contract. And my wife pointed out that I would still have to pay another £4,000 in a lump sum to own the car at the end of that time.*

> *"I looked online and found I could secure a personal loan now for about 10 per cent, which was much cheaper than the car finance. I asked the dealership what it would cost*

to buy our current slightly shabby car outright – they said £3,000 – which I thought was a chunky lump.

"Then, my wife showed me that during the five years we would be spending an extra £2,100 in interest on the upgrade, which was £9,600 in total. And we wouldn't even own the car at the end of it. But they made it sound so cheap 'only an extra £35 per month' seemed so reasonable. I don't think a new GPS and USB are worth that much. We can work around it. I want a car that nobody can repossess."

You can see from Roberto's example that sometimes you can't find another way without using financing for the assets you need initially. When his wife went through the totals, he realised how expensive the upgrade would be – even though it was sold to him as being 'only another £35 per month'. Understanding the terms of your finance is so important if you are going to be in control of your life and assets.

How best to pay off your debt

There are a variety of trustworthy theories about how best to pay off debt. Many people advise paying off the smallest debt first so you can simplify how many debts you have and enjoy an essential feeling of achievement.

This is often referred to as the snowball method of debt repayment.

Alternatively, you can pay off the most expensive debt first. That way, you reduce your interest expense as quickly as possible. If you have a secured debt – for example, a car or house loan – it is vital to maintain those debt payments to avoid repossession of anything you rely on to live in or travel to work.

Ultimately, it is up to you to decide, but I favour a blended approach.

If you can pay a debt off in two to three months by focusing on it – do it! Close those accounts as quickly as you can. Then, have another look at your remaining debts. If they each will take longer than three months to repay, overpay your most expensive debt first and make minimum payments on the others.

If you are struggling with debt and are confused by this information – please seek support. At the end of the chapter, I list organisations who can help you create a debt plan which works for your specific circumstances.

Know your debt and what you buy with it. The only person who benefits from you not understanding your debt is the lender. The time to have a good look at your debt terms is right now. Once again, I don't think you need to be perfect with the details but make sure you have the necessary information written down on paper so you know where it is.

For each of your debts, find out the following:

- how much you owe;

- what is the annual interest rate; and

- are there any assets that can be repossessed if you don't repay the debt?

Think about what you bought with that debt:

- do you still have that item now?;

- can you remember why you bought it?;

- was it an upgrade, an add-on, or a special package?; and

- if you need to sell that item, how much is it worth today?

Take your time to reflect on what you bought and whether you would rebuy it if you didn't already have it today. Without regret, consider what you might do differently.

Exercise – Understand Your Debt

Most people hold some debt they are too scared, confused or ashamed to look at. Don't let this be you. Use these simple prompts and write down the basics of your debt on paper.

This is one exercise where I recommend you ask your partner or a friend to help. They can search for the details and you can write them down.

1. Name of the debt

2. How much is still owing right now?

3. What is the yearly interest rate?

4. When is this debt due?

5. Do I need to pay anything more on the due date to get rid of the debt?

6. Is there security (e.g. a car) on this debt that can be repossessed?

7. How much are the payments per month?

8. My rating of the debt: good, bad or ugly

9. What I want to do with this debt

Dealing with debt is tricky but understand this, there is no perfect way. Ask a friend who you trust to help and make a pact to find out more about your debts together. Keep yourselves accountable and support each other. You will both be better for it.

Exercise – Revisit The Money Pizza Debt Slice

Look again at the Money Pizza in Chapter 1 and focus your attention on your debt, before answering the following questions, and writing down your answers:

- What do you think about the debt slice now?

- Do you understand more about how debt works?

- Are you comfortable with the debt that you hold?

- Rate yourself.

- What will your next step be in improving your score?

I F THERE IS ONE chapter which is the hardest to work through, I feel it might be this one. Struggling with debt can be a shameful experience. You may find yourself in a mental tug of war – thinking you are struggling, but unwilling to reach out for help. Understand you don't have to deal with debt alone and neither does seeking help commit you to one single course of action.

Talk to trusted friends or family for support, or contact the reputable debt support charities in your country. Be aware of schemes and scams that are promoted through social media channels and do your research. Remember, you can use debt wisely to help build your investments and assets – especially to purchase your home. You will be able to find your own way to balance your good and bad debts (if you have them)!

Recommended help with debt

United Kingdom

National Debtline – 0808 808 4000 –
https://nationaldebtline.org

StepChange Debt Charity – www.stepchange.org

Citizens Advice – www.citizensadvice.org.uk

CAP UK – https://capuk.org/get-help

Australia

National Debt Helpline – https://ndh.org.au

Way Forward Debt Relief Charity –
https://wayforward.org.au

New Zealand

Moneytalks helpline – 0800 345 123 –
www.moneytalks.co.nz

CAP NZ – www.capnz.org/get-help/debt-help

Your Money Pizza

Lucky Chapter Thirteen!

*"You've always had the power my dear, you
just had to learn it for yourself."*
Glinda, in The Wizard of Oz

H ELLO DEAR READER - what a fabulous and persistent
person you are!

You have made it so far and you're a fucking legend.
This is the highest possible praise you can get from an
Australian.

The truth is, not everyone will reach the end of this
book. Not everyone will see the point. There will be
many readers who rage that there is nothing new in
this book - that they knew it all already.

And that is... Entirely. The. Point.

You know in the film of the Wizard of Oz where Toto pulls back the curtain and the all-powerful wizard is revealed to be simply an old man? That his magic isn't that wonderful after all? I hope this book has been your big Wizard of Oz reveal. To be good with money, you need to have: basic arithmetic (and use a calculator to fill in the gaps); the willingness to ask questions; and trust in yourself so when you think something is not quite right, you know you can take action. That's all.

Reading this book and working through the exercises has given you a new tool in the Money Pizza which you can use to check in with yourself on your progress.

You are now better equipped to understand your motivations, values and goals. You know where your triggers for bad habits lie, and you have strategies to change them. You can review your finances without fear, and you know how to make great financial decisions. You can be more flexible with your money habits, and also have brave conversations to ask for what you want. You know how to tweak your behaviours to manage your outgoings, and build your own financial life preserver at the same time. Finally, you understand how to make investments that work for you and your lifestyle, as well as what to look out for when you use debt.

The magic is this: it's not what you know about money, but how you behave with it, that matters. (Forgive me if I sound like a broken record.) You may have already realised this book is less about giving you information, and more about giving you the tools to change your behaviour with money.

You now have all the information in your hands, and the capability in you, to change your money behaviour. From here on, it's up to you. Your choice could be to go looking for something else - that elusive secret sauce - that you believe lies somewhere out there.

Or, you could actually go and do all the things that this book recommends.

Trust yourself. You already have what you need to change your money behaviour. Now, it's about practicing those skills.

Put this book down and think. What's the first thing that you want to change in your money behaviour? What is one small step you can take to get yourself closer to that goal?

Does it, perhaps, involve having a conversation with someone? If you don't feel brave about having a money conversation - use this book as your excuse.

"My money coach says I should do it." That's the damn truth. Imagine a tiny version of me standing on your shoulder and squeaking, "JFDI[1] !" I'm cheering you on.

---

1. Just Fucking Do It – in case you were wondering.

Your conversation could start like this, "I want to make a change in my money situation and my money coach says I should talk about money more. Would you be willing to help me?"

If you are worried about what the response will be - now is the time to face your fears. What if the response is negative? What then? Well, that's certainly not ideal, but now you know you might want to look for support elsewhere.

Not everyone is going to enjoy talking about money and not everyone will want you to do it either.

The sad truth is, not everybody wants you to be empowered and in control of your finances. If you feel other people shutting you down when you are trying to make positive money changes, it is time to question their motives. I suspect they are not trying to keep you feeling safe, but are trying to make themselves feel safe.

Remember, when someone has control over your finances, they have control over you. So - who will be in control? You? I certainly hope so.

There is nothing fabulously new that you need to learn to be good with money. No secret ingredient or high-level accreditation is needed before you can make it. But there is a huge financial industry built on the premise that mere mortals cannot be trusted with their own money. It is bullshit.

You can be your own financial manager. You can be your own money coach. You have enough knowledge and experience to change your behaviours. This may feel like a really risky idea to you because you have never heard it before. But it is true.

The mark of a great coach is that when it comes to the performance, the race day or the competition, the coach melts into the background and disappears. The athlete or performer is completely empowered to do their thing alone, confident they have the skills to carry on without their coach by their side. I want the same thing for you.

You know what I would like? I would be so chuffed if this book were the only book you ever needed to change your money behaviour. I would love that the demand for my one-on-one services plummets, because my prospective clients read this book first and say, "That was fab, I don't need you any more, Fleur". That would be fucken' awesome.

All I can say now is this: go out and make a change. I know you can do it. You are ready.

With much sweary money love,

Fleur xxx

Contact the Author

If this book has helped you and you want to contact the author, please use the following channels to connect.

Email: fleur@wtf-money.com

Website: wtf-money.com

Subscribe to updates: wtf-money.com/newsletter

LinkedIn: Fleur Iannazzo

Instagram: @wtf.money.fleur @themoneypizza

Chapter by Chapter Quotation References

CHAPTER 1: HENRY ROLLINS (born 1961 and still alive and kicking) is a prolific singer, writer, comedian and activist. I was introduced to his work by a boyfriend when I was a teenager. I scoffed, because, with an intense stare, raspy voice, bulging muscles and tats everywhere, I thought he was a scary angry man. But I was very mistaken. He campaigns for human rights and against homophobia and his work is angry and hopeful. And he's a bit sweary.

Chapter 2: Carl Jung (1875-1961) was the founder of analytical psychology. Jung considered the main task of human development to be the lifelong process of differentiation of the self out of each individual's conscious and unconscious elements. His work has been hugely influential in how we think about psychiatry, anthropology, archaeology, literature, sociology, philosophy and religious studies.

Chapter 3: Roy E. Disney (1930-2009) was a long-time senior executive of the Walt Disney Company, which was founded by his uncle, Walt Disney and his father, Roy O. Disney.

Chapter 4: Hillel the Elder c.110BC was a philosopher, sage and scholar born in Babylon. The quote 'If not us, who? If not now, when?' is often attributed to John F. Kennedy, and has been repeated in many forms, not least by Emma Watson in her 2014 speech launching the UN's HeForShe campaign (She said: "If not me, who? If not now, when?"). However, it seems that Hillel said it first. In 27 words, he intelligently sums up what it means to be responsible, and also encourages us each to find our own path.

Chapter 5: Nelson Mandela (1918-2013) was a South African anti-apartheid and human rights activist. He was his county's first black head of state, and sought to foster racial reconciliation. And I'm sure he was talking about women, as well as men here in this quote.

Chapter 6: The good old Chinese Proverb has to make an appearance in these quotable quotes. I could not find the origin of this proverb – so if you know more about it, please let me know.

Chapter 7: Misty Copeland (born 1982 and still dancing) is an American ballet dancer and became the first African American woman to be promoted to principal dancer in the American Ballet Theatre's history. She was considered a prodigy who rose to stardom despite not starting ballet until the age of 13 – positively middle aged in the ballet world. As well as being a dancer, Misty is an entrepreneur, speaker and philanthropist.

Chapter 8: Joan Rivers (1933-2014) was a comedian, actress and writer, known for her blunt and controversial persona. She is considered a pioneer of women in comedy and would take no shit. She was an early supporter of HIV/AIDS activism movements and known as the City of San Diego's Joan of Arc for her philanthropic work. She was wealthy, bawdy and a force of nature. Just type 'Joan Rivers dirty laugh' into your search engine and see where it gets you!

Chapter 9: Seriously this is my original thought and I'm claiming it!

Chapter 10: Paulette Perhach wrote the viral online article, A Story of a Fuck Off Fund for the Billfold in 2016. It remains a combined wake up and call to action for all independent minded worker-bees who want something better for their lives. Read the full article here:

Chapter 11: Sir John Templeton (1912-2008) was a banker, investor, fund manager and philanthropist. He established an extremely successful mutual fund – the Templeton Growth Fund – and by listening to this one quote alone, you can avoid many common investing mistakes.

Chapter 12: Sammy Davis, Jr. (1925-1990) was an American singer, actor, comedian and dancer. He started at the age of three on the vaudeville circuit with his dad, Sammy David Snr. Davis was wildly popular and this popularity helped break down many barriers in the segregated American entertainment industry. Despite his huge career success, Davis died in debt to the US Internal Revenue Service.

Chapter 13: The character of the good witch, Glinda says this to Dorothy in the 1939 film version of The Wizard of Oz. The film production was problematic, not least due to the exploitation of Judy Garland who played the lead role. However, it communicated a key message from the books of the author L. Frank Baum, about personal empowerment and finding strength within oneself. Apt, really.

Extra Exercises

T HE FOLLOWING EXERCISES ARE provided here if you want
to do some extra reflection. Not every chapter has
extra exercises, but you will find that these reflections
will enhance your awareness of your attitudes towards
money. They are completely optional and designed to
add to the work you have already done in the main part
of the book.

Chapter 2 – Your Money Story

Visualisation - Money Inner Child

If you found the First Money Experiences exercise
painful, or it made you sad, use the following
visualisation.

Find a safe place for yourself where you won't be
interrupted for 10 minutes.

Imagine you are able to go back in time to that young person you pictured in the First Money Experiences exercise.

They need your support and as you look back in time, you realise that this person is doing the very best they can with what they have at that moment.

You feel compassion rising up within you, and you want to comfort them.

In your mind's eye, reach out and hold their hand.

If you want to say something kind to them, do so. Say it out loud if it helps.

Then, imagine an ending to the scene which gives you a positive resolution. Maybe, you carry the child away to a safe place. Maybe, you walk together and have a meaningful conversation.

It's up to you how the story ends. Sit with the ending for a while, and notice how you feel.

First Money Conversations Exercise

Think back to the household where you grew up. Was money spoken about openly? If not, how did you learn about the concept of money? Were there any emotions or actions which were associated with money, including: pride; shame; success; achievement; comparison ... etc?

Write down as much as you can remember.

What does this tell you about yourself and how you talk about money today?

Chapter 3 – Your Money Compass

Exercise – The Team of You

Think about the different roles you play in life. These can be work related, family related, as a dependent, or as a care giver. Or, like a certain pop group you might have: Sporty You; Glamour You; Scary You; Baby You; Career You; Intellectual You; Cosplay You, and so on. Remember to identify your ideal role – the person you want to be – because that is an important part of you too.

Give each of these roles or characters a name. Then imagine that you are all sitting down around a table together having a discussion. Notice how each character looks, talks, and behaves. Ask each character to finish the following sentence.

My ideal financial life is like this …

Write down each of their statements.

Consider what has come out on the paper.

As your unified whole person, finish this sentence: The meaningful messages I take from these statements are ...

Once you have done that, take a deep breath and imagine you are sitting back at the table with your different characters. Go around again and ask them each to finish this sentence: Teamwork In this wonderful life of ours means ...

If this resonates with you, write down this teamwork statement somewhere you can refer to it easily.

Consider the last time you made an important financial decision and which of the characters were involved in the decision.

Did one dominate and crowd out the others?

What was the benefit of this?

What were the drawbacks?

What does this tell you about how you have been making your financial decisions?

Exercise – Uncover Your Beliefs

Take some time for yourself in a private place where you can be alone with your thoughts. Think about a scenario where you have acted in a way which ultimately held you back, or you did something which you later regretted. Perhaps you stayed quiet while someone bullied a friend –

you might believe conflict is bad - or to be involved would put you in danger. Take time to sit with each thought and ask yourself if there is something else that lies underneath the memory.

Are you aware of any seemingly random thoughts, which pop into your head when you are doing this?

What do those thoughts and pictures tell you?

Do you feel challenged by something? Perhaps you cannot bring yourself to ask for a pay rise. What is driving this behaviour?

When you imagine doing the challenging thing, what thoughts about yourself and the world pop into your head?

There is no perfect way to complete this exercise. You may experience an 'Aha!' moment instantly – or it may take more time to work out what these things mean for you. Do not worry, you can always revisit this exercise, and there is no rush.

Chapter 6 - Great Financial Decisions

Exercise – Future Focus

Sometimes we are faced with a decision that is uncomfortable in the short term, but provides longer-term benefits to ourselves. This exercise helps you focus on the longer-term outcomes.

Your older-self (and wiser-self) travels back in time to have a hot drink and a conversation with you. What does that older-self want you to do right now? What are they proud of you for doing? What do they wish for you right now?

Now, ask that older-self: What would you like me to do for you right now? What decision do you want me to take? Why do you want me to make this decision?

Note down any thoughts or ideas that you have.

References, Research and Resources

Chapter 1 – What is the Money Pizza?

THINKING, FAST AND SLOW, Daniel Kahneman, Macmillan, 2011.

Nudge: Improving Decisions About Health, Wealth and Happiness, Richard H. Thaler and Cass R. Sunstein, Penguin, 2008.

Elinor Ostrom
https://www.nobelprize.org/prizes/economic-sciences/2009/ostrom/biographical/

Mr Spock is Not As Logical As He'd Like to Think, Tim Harford
https://timharford.com/2021/07/me-spock-is-not-as-logical-as-hed-like-to-think/ - published 21 July 2021.

Not In Your Genes: The real reasons children are like their parents, Oliver James, Vermillion Press, 2016.

Chapter 2 – Your Money Story

Habit Formation and Learning in Young Children, Dr David Whitebread and Dr Sue Bingham, University of Cambridge, Published by the Money Advice Service (now known as the Money & Pensions Service), UK Government, released May 2013, Available athttps://maps.org.uk/wp-content/uploads/2021/03/the-money-advice-service-habit-formation-and-learning-in-young-children-may-2013.pdf [Accessed May 2022].

Chapter 3 – Your Money Compass

The Winding Roads to Adulthood: A Twin Study, Kaili Rimfeld, Margherita Malanchini, Amy E. Packer, Agnieszka Gidziela, Andrea G. Allegrini, Ziada Ayorech, Emily Smith-Woolley, Andrew McMillan, Rachel Ogden, Philip S. Dale, Thalia C. Eley and Robert Plomin. Journal of Child Psychology and Psychiatry, November 2021. Available at https://acamh.onlinelibrary.wiley.com/doi/epdf/10.1002/jcv2.12053 [Accessed May 2022]

Cognitive Behavioural Therapy for Dummies – Portable Edition – Rhena Branch and Rob Wilson, Wiley, 2011.

Motivational Interviewing: Helping People Change, 3rd Edition, William R. Miller and Stephen Rollnick, Guildford Press, 2013.

Coaching Athletes to Be Their Best: Motivational Interviewing in Sports, Stephen Rollnick, Jonathan Fader, Jeff Breckton, and Theresa B. Moyers, Guildford Press, 2020.

Chapter 4 – Money Dramas

Open Up: The Power of Talking About Money, Alex Holder, Serpent's Tail, 2019.

TA Today: A New Introduction to Transactional Analysis, 2nd Edition by Ian Stewart and Vann Joines, Lifespace Publishing, 2012.

Chapter 5 – Fearless Financial Review

Emotions Revealed: Understanding Faces and Feelings, Paul Ekman, London: Weidenfeld & Nicolson, 2003.

Made of Stronger Stuff – BBC Sounds
https://www.bbc.co.uk/programmes/p094py21

Chapter 6 – Great Financial Decisions

Why Has Nobody Told Me This Before? Dr Julie Smith, Penguin Random House, 2022.

Chapter 7 – Financial Flexibility

Ageing and strategic learning: The impact of spousal incentives on financial literacy, J. W. Hsu (2016) *Journal of Human Resources,* Issue 51, pages 1036-1067.

Worldwide Cost of Living 2021: explore the rise and fall of living costs in 173 cities. Economist Intelligence Unit, available at https://www.eiu.com/n/campaigns/worldwide-cost-of-living-2021/?utm_source=economist&utm_medium=daily_chart&utm_campaign=wcol21 [Accessed 21 November 2022]

Chapter 8 – Ask For What You Want

Negotiation Genius: How to Overcome Obstacles and Achieve Brilliant Results at the Bargaining Table and Beyond, Deepak Malhorta and Max Bazerman, Penguin Random House, 2008.

Ask For It: How Women Can Use The Power of Negotiation To Get What They Really Want, Linda Babcock and Sara Laschever, Random House, 2008.

*Behavioural Responses to Stress in Females: Tend-and-Befriend, Not Fight-or-Fligh*t, Shelley E. Taylor, Laura Cousino Klein, Brian P. Lewis, Tara L. Gruenewald, Tegan A. R. Gruning and John A. Updegraff of the University of California, Los Angeles. Published in the

Psychological Review, 2000, Volume 107, Issue Number 3, pages 411-429.

Chapter 9 – Manage Your Outgoings

Why Saving is like Dieting and Budgets Don't Work, Susan Jackson, The Women's Financial Network, 2004.

Alchemy: The Magic of Original Thinking in a World of Mind-Numbing Conformity, Rory Sutherland, Penguin, 2021.

Mindset: Changing the Way You Think to Fulfil Your Potential, Dr Carol Dweck, Random House, 2006.

The Barefoot Investor for Families, Scott Pape, HarperCollins Publishers, 2020.

You're Not Broke You're Pre Rich: How to Make Your Money Work For You, Emilie Bellet, Hachette, 2019.

Chapter 10 – Build Your Financial Life Preserver

Paulette Perhach wrote a blog article for the Billfold in 2016, which went viral for good reason. She has been cited repeatedly ever since. But her blog is a great one and will get you fired up. Read the original article from this link
https://www.thebillfold.com/2016/01/a-story-of-a-fuck-off-f-fund/

Chapter 11 – Strategic Investments

A great way to start educating yourself about investments is to listen to reputable podcasts from financial publications. Try *Money Clinic* with Claer Barrett from the Financial Times: https://www.ft.com/money-clinic-with-claer-barrett

Chapter 12 – How to Use Debt Wisely

Debt: The First 5,000 Years, David Graeber, This is an incredibly great book about how debt has developed and its implications for society that run so deeply we barely notice them. David Graeber is a professor of Anthropology (the study of Humanity) at the London School of Economics, UK.

Acknowledgements

Thanks first and foremost to Wendy Yorke, without whom I would never have managed to finish the manuscript for this, my very first book.

Thank you to the MSc12 cohort of the Masters in Coaching and Behavioural Change at Henley Business School. Your jokes, encouragement and willingness to be fellow shit-stirrers gave me strength to be myself as a coach and follow my own path.

I would not have survived without my study group: Iris Ben-Gal Madsen, Sarah Lawrence, Edina Dobos, Aga Laherto and Priscilla Filleti. Thank you for your support through all the wibbles and wobbles of the MSc dissertation. Our continuing weekly check ins kept me going through this bigger writing project.

There is a library in heaven for the beta-readers who generously read, commented on and proof-read the manuscript: Donna Price, Cam-Tu Tomkins, Charlie Clarey, David Stirling, Carla Hoppe, Garry Browne, Michelle Hall,

Lizzie Blaxland, Di Binley, Erica Leyshon and Lizzie Shi. I didn't think The Money Pizza was a viable project until you gave me your feedback and your faith.

Special mention to the eagle-eyed Kate Scott and Garret Tynan. Thank you for every comma, comment and suggestion. Any unreadable phrases, spelling mistakes or loose language is because I chose to wilfully ignore your good advice.

Thank you to Jane, for helping me realise what a success it is to write a book and put it out there. To Nicola and Matilda for the Friday evening get togethers which keep me sane.

Endless thanks to Jonathan Cantwell for all the times you noticed me glued to the computer screen and handed me food and drinks without expecting any eye contact or response. You gave me the space and support which I didn't know I needed - and kept the chocolate coming.

And finally to Vanessa. Thank you for being the inspiration to make the change I want to see in the world.

About the Author

Fleur Iannazzo is a recovering banker and a money psychologist who is determined to help everyone change the way they think and behave with their money.

Having spent 18 years working in financial services, Fleur understands that even finance professionals struggle with money issues. For more than 25 years Fleur has also been a rowing coach. One day she realised that she could use her coaching experience to help people change what they do with their money.

Fleur is a Chartered Financial Analyst and holds a MSc in Coaching and Behavioural Change from Henley Business School. In 2020, she established her own business in London, WTF Money, providing one-to-one coaching to help professionals navigate their own financial shit storms.

Photo credit: Jackie Rado Photography

After growing up in Melbourne, Australia and spending a decade working in Hong Kong, Fleur now works and lives in London. Every now and then she raids her swear jar and goes travelling.

You can email her at fleur@wtf-money.com